RUGBY
WORLD CUP '95

THIS IS A CARLTON BOOK

This edition first published in 1995

1 2 3 4 5 6 7 8 9 10

Text and design copyright © Carlton Books Limited 1995

First published in the United Kingdom in 1995 by
Aurum Press Limited, 25 Bedford Avenue, London WC1B 3AT

A catalogue record for this book is available from the British Library

ISBN 1 85410 348 2

Project Editor: **Martin Corteel**
Project art direction: **Robert Fairclough**
Editor: **David Ballheimer**
Designer: **Daniel Duke**
Picture research: **Charlotte Bush**
Production: **Sarah Schuman**

Printed and bound in Great Britain

THE AUTHOR

Richard Bath is the editor of *Rugby News* magazine. He also writes for *The Sunday Times* and was co-editor of the official guide to the World Cup Sevens. He has written widely through the national press in Britain and for most specialist rugby publications throughout the world.

RUGBY WORLD CUP '95

Richard Bath

Editor of *Rugby News* magazine

AURUM PRESS

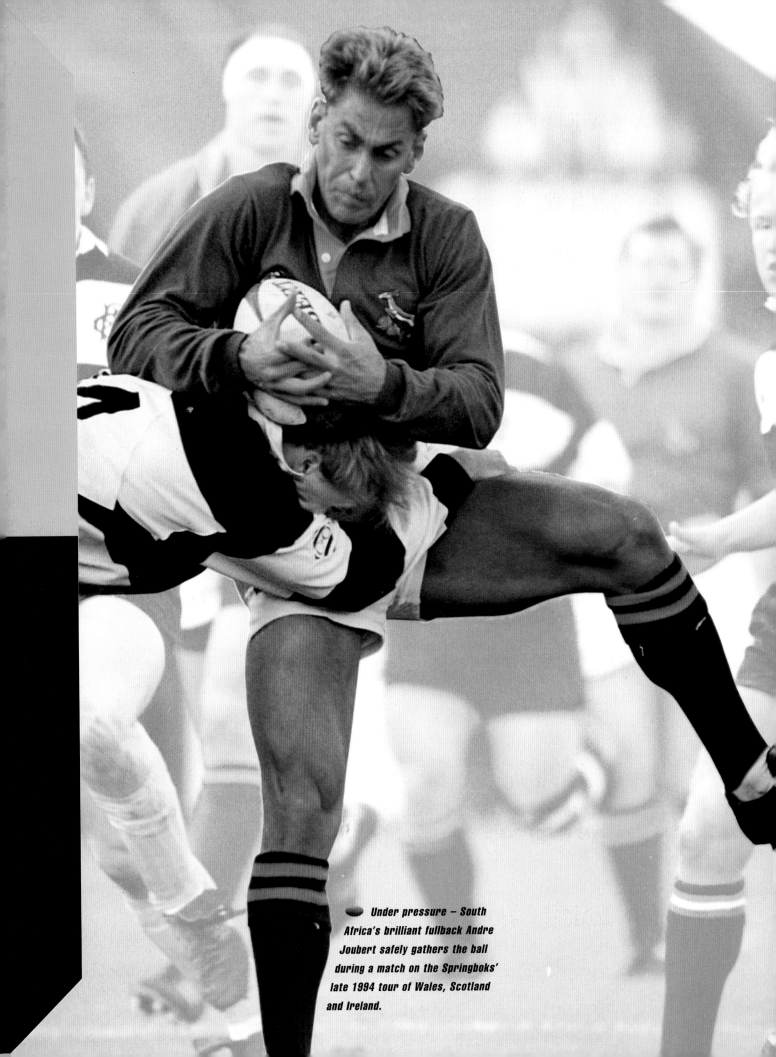

Under pressure – South Africa's brilliant fullback Andre Joubert safely gathers the ball during a match on the Springboks' late 1994 tour of Wales, Scotland and Ireland.

CONTENTS

A Festival of Dazzling RUGBY

Rugby has come of age – and it is all because of the tremendous power of the World Cup. In eight years, the face of the game has been changed forever by the catalytic effect of one of the world's most popular sporting events. The focus of the rugby world's attention has now shifted irrevocably from the passionate but mainly parochial interest in the Five Nations and the Bledisloe Cup to the all-consuming lure of the game's Holy Grail – the contest for the Webb Ellis Trophy.

Bok with a vengeance – Springbok fans had little to cheer about during the first two World Cups, but the hosting of the 1995 event in South Africa has made the competition even more eagerly awaited.

Once an insular, closed sport in which only history counted for anything, rugby has now become a world sport. Before the first World Cup, the game's governing body, the International Rugby Football Board, numbered only 17 members. Entering 1995, that number stood at 67, and climbing, as countries new to the game signed up for their shot at the big time as a World Cup qualifier.

> *The tournament will provide a festival of dazzling rugby, friendship and sunshine.*
>
> **LOUIS LUYT,**
> South Africa's organiser-in-chief of the
> 1995 Rugby World Cup

And not only are more people playing the game, but more are watching; only 17 countries took televised coverage of the 1987 event, 103 showed the 1991 tournament and there will be closer to 150 in South Africa. An idea that was realised by the late John Kendall-Carpenter in the mid 1980s, the Rugby World Cup has now consolidated its position as one of the sport's greatest treasures.

While the 1987 and 1991 tournaments were huge successes, 1995 in South Africa should go down as an even greater tournament. In the lead up to the Finals, South Africa's World Cup organiser Louis Luyt predicted: "You will see the most spectacular success and an awful lot of money will be made." The host country certainly has a rugby-mad population, huge stadiums and all the facilities to make this one of the great sporting events, while the inclusion of the Springboks fills the gaping credibility hole that has existed since South Africa were excluded from the first two tournaments. Now the winners of the tournament will never be in any doubt that they are indeed the best in the world.

LOOKING BACK

Memories come flooding back when fans look back at 1987 and '91. Who can forget Serge Blanco's last-gasp dash to beat Australia in the '87 Semi-final, or John Kirwan's swerving, side-stepping 80-yard blast through 11 Italian tackles as the All Blacks won their opening game by a crushing 70–6 margin? And what about 1991, with Gordon Hamilton and Michael Lynagh's tries in the Ireland v Australia Quarter-final – one of the most exciting games ever played – or the Wallabies' magical Semi-final display when they blitzed holders New Zealand?

Yet come 25 June 1995, there will be new memories to relive, new heroes to fete and new powers to have emerged in the fastest growing team sport in the world. So, roll on Cape Town and the earth-shaking opening clash between hosts South Africa and defending champions Australia!

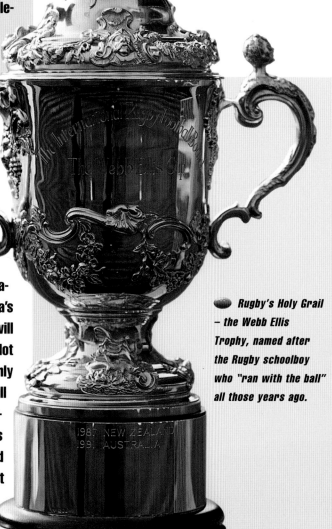

Rugby's Holy Grail – the Webb Ellis Trophy, named after the Rugby schoolboy who "ran with the ball" all those years ago.

The 1995 World Cup
FINALS

There was a great deal of debate after South Africa was chosen to host the 1995 World Cup. The feeling persisted that the country, then still trying to implement its promise to abolish Apartheid, was just not stable enough to hold a major world tournament. There was also a fear that the competition would be hijacked by political factions hoping to use it for their own ends.

Three years on, the situation has completely changed. While the society still has many problems, disorder in the townships does not daily fill television screens around the world, and the white community has fulfilled its promise to abolish Apartheid and started to build a society that reflects the country's multi-racial population.

More to the point, the tournament is now seen as a major unifying influence in South Africa, and has attracted the wholehearted support of both black and white power brokers. As well as a massive influx of foreign currency, it is also hoped that the event will give the rest of the world an opportunity to see how professionally the new South Africa can work.

And there can be fewer better places to hold a major tournament such as the World Cup. Rugby is still something of a religion in South Africa, and interest in the tournament will be all-consuming for the whole of May and June. South Africa also boasts the best rugby stadiums in the world – there are few arenas in world sport which can compare to Loftus Versfeld, Newlands or Ellis Park.

PLAYING WITH THE ELEMENTS

But while South Africa has much to offer, it also has elements which make defeating the home country very difficult. The Highvelt in the north of the country is so far above sea level that it means sides playing there will fade dramatically late in the game unless they take stringent measures to make sure they are fully acclimatised.

Another feature that sets South Africa apart is the rock hard grounds upon which the game is played. It makes the game so much faster than that played on the softer ground of, say, Britain, that the game takes on a different tactical shape, as England discovered to their cost on the tour there in May and June 1994. As well as putting greater emphasis on running with the ball rather than keeping it tight, the hard grounds also make kicking more effective, particularly at altitude, where the thin air allows the ball to fly further than it does at sea level. This combination has helped to produce some of rugby's greatest kickers – like the former Springbok fly-half Naas Botha.

This all makes South Africa ideal World Cup hosts: it has a warm, sunny climate; wonderful stadia; knowledgeable fans; hosts sure to do well; it is a relatively cheap country in which to stay and travel and its hard grounds make for exciting open rugby.

Rugby in the townships is still at a developmental stage, and equipment remains at a premium. However, there is enormous enthusiasm with children finally getting a chance to show their talents. They benefit from the extra freedom that allows coaches to go into the townships to properly teach the rudiments of the game.

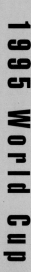

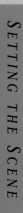

South Africa's Rugby
COLOSSEUMS

The 1995 Rugby World Cup will be the first to be held exclusively in one single country, and there could be no more fitting country in which to hold the event. Quite simply, South Africa has the best stadia and the most impressive rugby infra-structure in the world. England may have Twickenham, France may have the Parc des Princes and New Zealand may have Eden Park, but no other country has the sheer number of top quality venues that South Africa possesses.

The fanatical following the country's domestic Currie Cup competition has attracted for many years now has also ensured full houses week in, week out for the top six provinces. Add in hefty state subsidies and tax breaks and the result is a collection of magnificent stadia which make the perfect set of venues for the third World Cup.

Every major ground in South Africa has a story to tell, but whether it is the damp sea-level surface at Newlands, or the baked hard cricket square of the Orange Free State, there is one thing for certain — that the rich variety of venues in South Africa will provide the best possible showcase for the game.

Bloemfontein

LOCATION: Free State Stadium, Bloemfontein, Orange Free State
CAPACITY: 36,500
HISTORY: Bloemfontein is right at the heart of South Africa, both metaphorically and geographically. The predominantly open-air stadium, with its rock-hard pitch, is famous for producing open running rugby. In the process of major redevelopment expected to be finished on May 1, 1995.

Stellenbosch

LOCATION: Danie Craven Stadium, Stellenbosch, Western Cape
CAPACITY: 17,500
HISTORY: Stellenbosch is the site of one of the world's most famous universities, and that is the way in which the ground receives most use. The stadium is open-air, in keeping with the town's relaxed, sunny and peaceful aura. It is home to the Craven/Markotter Rugby Museum.

Port Elizabeth

LOCATION: Boet Erasmus, Port Elizabeth, Eastern Cape
CAPACITY: 34,000
HISTORY: Port Elizabeth, the "friendly city", is the most English of cities in South Africa. A quaint, relaxed environment on the coast, the ground is as much a strange amalgam of the new and the old as the city itself. Boet Erasmus has excellent facilities, but is mostly uncovered.

Cape Town

LOCATION: Newlands, Cape Town, Western Cape
CAPACITY: 51,000
HISTORY: Lying in the Cape Town suburb of Newlands, Western Province's stadium is the oldest in the country (built in1888) and is almost certainly the most beautiful of the major venues. Nestling at the foot of Table Mountain and overlooking the sea, it is the only stadium where the ground can get damp enough to resemble European conditions.

Rustenburg

LOCATION: Olympia Park Stadium, Rustenburg, North-West

CAPACITY: 32,000

HISTORY: Probably one of the most beautiful stadia in the rugby world. Located in the lush sub-tropical area in the north of the country that is the gateway to Sun City, the open air stadium is ultra-modern – with the exception of the East Pavilion, a stand which originally came fromLoftus Versfeld.

Pretoria

LOCATION: Loftus Versfeld, Pretoria, Pretoria-Witwatersrand-Vereeniging

CAPACITY: 53,000

HISTORY: One of the four permanent Test stadiums in the country, Loftus Versfeld is famous for being far above sea level. Situated four miles out of Pretoria, the ground is next to Pretoria University (the world's largest rugby club – it fields over 60 teams each week!)

Johannesburg

LOCATION: Ellis Park, Johannesburg, PWV

CAPACITY: 80,000

HISTORY: The venue for the 1995 Rugby World Cup final. Ellis Park is another of the stadia where altitude is a consideration and is being renovated in an attempt to push the capacity up to 80,000. It is also a beautiful stadium, and is home to Currie Cup champions Transvaal. Situated right in the centre of capital city Johannesburg.

East London

LOCATION: Basil Kenyon Stadium, East London, Eastern Cape

CAPACITY: 19,000

HISTORY: Named after the famous 1950's Springbok captain from the Border region, this stadium is one of the oldest in the country – and looks like it! One of the last to retain a sizeable standing capacity, it is very reminiscent of a New Zealand ground, and is almost completely exposed to the elements.

Durban

LOCATION: Kings Park, Durban, KwaZulu Natal

CAPACITY: 51,000

HISTORY: Durban has a very high average temperature (18-23°C) and is very humid. Kings Park is just outside the city and is one of the most impressive stadia in the country. It has also undergone major renovation and backs on to the sea. Kings Park is famous for its after-match "Bries" (barbeques) on the surrounding grounds.

THE LUCK OF
THE DRAW

With sixteen countries qualifying for the 1995 World Cup, competition was always going to be fierce. The first eight places went to the quarter-finalists from 1991 – England, France, New Zealand, Canada, Australia, Ireland, Western Samoa and Scotland – while the ninth went to the hosts, South Africa. That left seven qualifiers to emerge from the seven pools – Europe West, Europe Central, Europe East, Asia, The Pacific, The Americas and Africa.

South Africa's Sports Minister Steve Tshwete – who played rugby at the notorious Robben Island jail – with the World Cup.

The result was four groups for South Africa with two "seeds" (i.e. two quarter-finalists from 1991) and two qualifiers. These were then sectioned off geographically with each pool centred around two or three venues and then played on a round-robin basis with two points for a win and one for a draw.

🏉 POOL A – THE POOL OF DEATH

With hosts South Africa joining champions Australia in this group, this may be the most keenly contested pool of all. Australia and South Africa are the two favourites for the tournament and their meeting in the opening game is a marketing man's dream. After their remarkable progress in 1991, Canada deserved a fairer chance of qualifying for the quarter-finals. As it is, neither they nor Romania have much chance of progressing beyond their group. But with two of the most rugged packs in world rugby, there can be little doubt that they will both prove to be exceptionally tough opponents for South Africa and Australia.

🏉 POOL B – TOO CLOSE TO CALL

England will start as warm favourites in this group, and should win all three Pool games. Western Samoa may have come a long way, but they will not match England's power at the set-pieces, while much the same goes for Argentina and Italy. Who qualifies with England, however, is harder to guess. Western Samoa have lost some key players from the last World Cup, while Argentina – who almost overcame the Samoans in 1991 – have beaten Scotland and France since 1993. Italy have also come on strong in 1993–94, and almost beat world champions Australia in both tests when they toured there.

🏉 POOL C – CELTIC DOGFIGHT

Memories of 1987 will come flooding back for Wales. They were overwhelmed 49–6 by New Zealand in the 1987 World Cup semi-final, a match which marked the start of a downward spiral from which they are only now emerging. New Zealand should win this pool, notwithstanding Ireland's

ability to pull off a shock win when they are least expected to. Japan will be outclassed, but probably not embarrassed by either Wales or Ireland. Pool C will eventually come down to one match: that between Wales and Ireland, which will dictate who goes through with New Zealand.

🏉 POOL D – GALLIC TOUR DE FORCE

France are dark horses for the tournament, and they will be hot favourites in this Pool. The chances of either Scotland, Tonga or Ivory Coast topping the group look remote. Scotland prefer softer grounds, but should have too much experience and class for both Tonga (although the Scottish Development team was well beaten on their Pacific Islands tour in 1992) and the Ivory Coast, who they have never met. Tonga and the Ivory Coast are likely to contest the wooden spoon place in this group, but their powerful forwards may sap much of the two pool favourites' strength for later in the tournament.

🏉 THE KNOCK-OUT ROUNDS

The quarter-finals onwards will provide some fascinating contests. The first should see France go through against either Wales or Ireland, while Australia will probably meet Western Samoa, which can only be bad news for the Samoans, who conceded over 70 points when they met the Wallabies in a decidedly one-sided contest in July 1994. The third quarter-final could be the most intriguing. England have shown they can beat South Africa, but the home side traditionally have such an advantage that England will do very well indeed to survive through to the semi-final stage. The last quarter-final, expected to be between New Zealand and Scotland, should be a re-run of the 1991 third-place play-off when the All Blacks' dominance was not reflected in a 13–6 scoreline. This should lead to semi-finals pitting France against defending champions Australia, in a repeat of the fantastic 1987 semi-final at the Concord Oval in Sydney, and South Africa against the '87 champions New Zealand. Then, on 24 June, at Ellis Park, Johannesburg, the 1995 World Cup winners will be crowned.

HOW THEY LINE UP

POOL A	POOL B	POOL C	POOL D
Australia	*England*	*New Zealand*	*France*
South Africa	*Western Samoa*	*Ireland*	*Scotland*
Canada	*Argentina*	*Wales*	*Tonga*
Romania	*Italy*	*Japan*	*Ivory Coast*
Venues	**Venues**	**Venues**	**Venues**
CAPE TOWN	EAST LONDON	JOHANNESBURG	PRETORIA
PORT ELIZABETH	DURBAN	BLOEMFONTEIN	RUSTENBURG
STELLENBOSCH			

The Long Trek to
RUGBY NIRVANA

Chart the progress of the 1995 World Cup on these two pages, so that at the end you will have a record of the key events of the tournament, and a lasting memento of the winners and losers from South Africa 1995.

In the first round there are four pools, from which the first and second teams in each group proceed to the quarter-finals. Space has been allowed for you to fill in the scores of the matches and the final placings in each pool. After the first round, the competition follows a straight knock-out system. The teams will not be known until the pool games are completed, but we indicate which pool winners and runners-up will play, when and where, all the way through to the third and fourth-place play-off in Pretoria and the Final at Ellis Park in Johannesburg on June 24. Space has again been provided for you to fill in the teams and the scores for each match, as well as the points scorers in the final itself.

First Round

Pool A

		Score
Thur, May 25 (Cape Town)	Australia vs. South Africa (3.30 p.m.)	....
Fri, May 26 (Port Elizabeth)	Canada vs. Romania (8.00 p.m.)	....
Tue, May 30 (Cape Town)	South Africa vs. Romania (2.30 p.m.)	....
Wed, May 31 (Port Elizabeth)	Australia vs. Canada (1.00 p.m.)	....
Sat, June 3 (Stellenbosch)	Australia vs. Romania (3.00 p.m.)	....
Sat, June 3 (Port Elizabeth)	Canada vs. South Africa (8.00 p.m.)	....

FINAL TABLE P W D L F A Pts

1 ....
2 ....
3 ....
4 ....

Pool B

		Score
Sat, May 27 (East London)	Western Samoa vs. Italy (1.00 p.m.)	....
Sat, May 27 (Durban)	England vs. Argentina (5.00 p.m.)	....
Tue, May 30 (East London)	Western Samoa vs. Argentina (12.30 p.m.)	....
Wed, May 31 (Durban)	England vs. Italy (5.00 p.m.)	....
Sun, June 4 (East London)	Argentina vs. Italy (1.00 p.m.)	....
Sun, June 4 (Durban)	England vs. Western Samoa (8.00 p.m.)	....

FINAL TABLE P W D L F A Pts

1 ....
2 ....
3 ....
4 ....

Pool C

		Score
Sat, May 27 (Bloemfontein)	Wales vs. Japan (3.00 p.m.)	....
Sat, May 27 (Johannesburg)	New Zealand vs. Ireland (8.00 p.m.)	....
Wed, May 31 (Bloemfontein)	Ireland vs. Japan (3.00 p.m.)	....
Wed, May 31 (Johannesburg)	New Zealand vs. Wales (8.00 p.m.)	....
Sun, June 4 (Bloemfontein)	New Zealand vs. Japan (3.00 p.m.)	....
Sun, June 4 (Johannesburg)	Ireland vs. Wales (5.00 p.m.)	....

FINAL TABLE P W D L F A Pts

1 ....
2 ....
3 ....
4 ....

Pool D

		Score
Fri, May 26 (Rustenburg)	Scotland vs. Ivory Coast (4.00 p.m.)	....
Fri, May 26 (Pretoria)	France vs. Tonga (6.00 p.m.)	....
Tue, May 30 (Rustenburg)	France vs. Ivory Coast (6.00 p.m.)	....
Tue, May 30 (Pretoria)	Scotland vs. Tonga (8.00 p.m.)	....
Sat, June 3 (Rustenburg)	Tonga vs. Ivory Coast (1.00 p.m.)	....
Sat, June 3 (Pretoria)	Scotland vs. France (5.00 p.m.)	....

FINAL TABLE P W D L F A Pts

1 ....
2 ....
3 ....
4 ....

Quarter-Finals

Saturday June 10 (1.00 p.m.)
Winners Pool D vs. Runners-up Pool C (Durban – E)

....

Saturday June 10 (3.30 p.m.)
Winners Pool A vs. Runners-up Pool B (Johannesburg – F)

....

Sunday June 11 (1.00 p.m.)
Winners Pool B vs. Runners-up Pool A (Cape Town – H)

....

Sunday June 11 (3.30 p.m.)
Winners Pool C vs. Runners-up Pool D (Pretoria – G)

....

Semi-Finals

Saturday June 17 (3.00 p.m.)
Winners Durban quarter-final (E) vs.
Winners Johannesburg quarter-final (F) (Durban)

....

Sunday June 18 (3.00 p.m.)
Winners Pretoria quarter-final (G) vs.
Winners Cape Town quarter-final (H) (Cape Town)

....

Third-Place Play-Off

Thursday June 22 (5.00 p.m.)
Pretoria

....

....

The Final

Saturday June 24 (3.00 p.m.)
Johannesburg

....

Scorers   Scorers

....

....

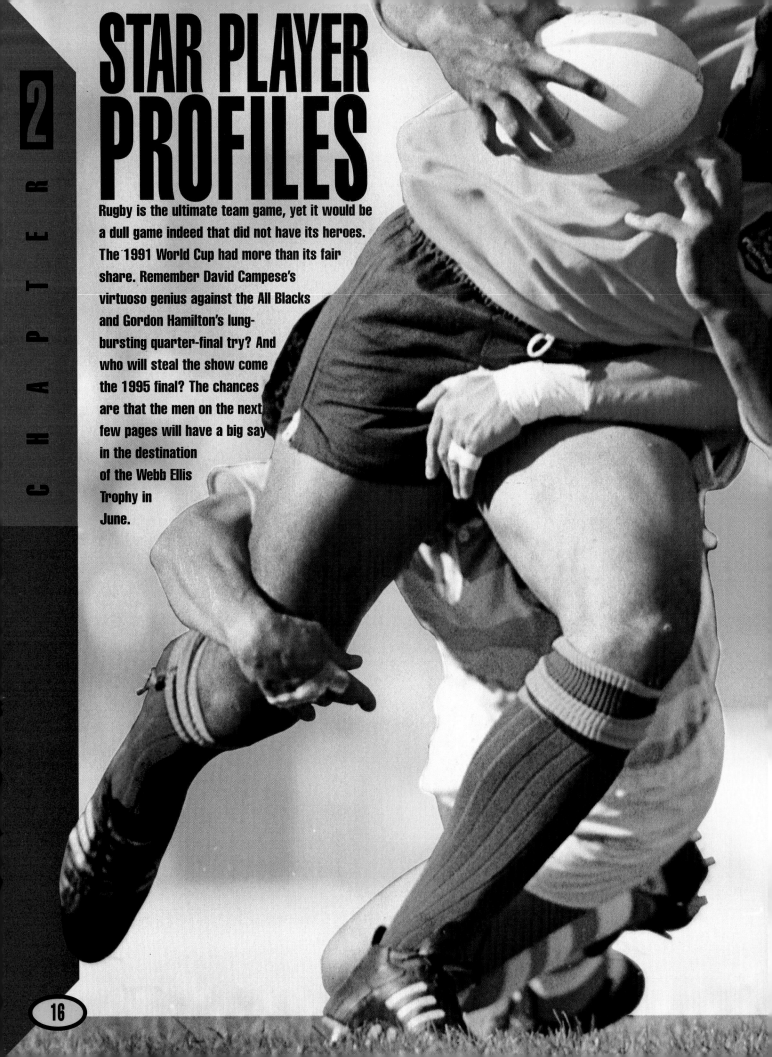

CHAPTER 2

STAR PLAYER PROFILES

Rugby is the ultimate team game, yet it would be a dull game indeed that did not have its heroes. The 1991 World Cup had more than its fair share. Remember David Campese's virtuoso genius against the All Blacks and Gordon Hamilton's lung-bursting quarter-final try? And who will steal the show come the 1995 final? The chances are that the men on the next few pages will have a big say in the destination of the Webb Ellis Trophy in June.

From Sevens to All Black Eight ZINZAN
BROOKE

It is rare indeed for New Zealand players – let alone forwards – to start life as Sevens players and then move into the 15-a-side game rather than the other way around. Yet that is how Zinzan Brooke got his big break.

A naturally gifted ball player, it was those attributes most evident when he played sevens for which he quickly became best known. Even if the All Blacks of the mid to late Eighties were often in expansive mode, Brooke found it difficult to shake the impression that he did not have a sufficiently tight game to graduate to the All Blacks.

Not so says former New Zealand coach John Hart, who coached Brooke at Auckland. "Zinny's punishing tackling – he excels in front-on defence – and excellent catching and kicking ability make him a complete defensive player, but he also has the strength to go over the gain line and the skill to distribute well."

Making his debut in 1987, against Argentina, Brooke was unfortunate to have come on the scene when Buck Shelford was in full cry. There was no shifting the great man – who, remarkably, won every game as

Zinzan Brooke – a great ball-handler with a surprising turn of pace.

> "Zinzan is one of the most talented players I have ever worked with."

JOHN HART,
FORMER AUCKLAND AND
NEW ZEALAND COACH

New Zealand's captain – so Brooke had to wait another two years until he won another cap, again against Argentina, and it wasn't until 1990, when Shelford was surprisingly dropped, that Brooke's All Black career took off in earnest.

Since then, the Auckland captain has proved himself one of the outstanding number 8s in world rugby. Rugged and hard-tackling, he retains the great hands that characterised his sevens career and is an astute reader of a game.

He suffered from being thought not sufficiently robust going forward, and coach Laurie Mains tried out other contenders. He lost his place to Arran Pene for a while, regained it, and became one of the few All Blacks whose place was not under threat after the New Zealanders had, by Kiwi standards, a profoundly disappointing 1994 season.

He now finds himself playing in an All Black shirt alongside younger brother Robin, a lock, while another, older, brother, Marty, was an All Black triallist.

Zinzan Brooke

BORN:	14 February 1965 Waiuku
CLUBS:	Marist and Auckland
DEBUT:	vs. Argentina, 1987
HEIGHT:	6ft 3in (1.91m)
WEIGHT:	15st 9lb (85kg)
JOB:	Courier

ZINZAN'S middle name is Valentine but he's one person who's never happy to see a bunch of red roses!

The Wizard from Oz DAVID CAMPESE

There is no bigger draw in world rugby than the world's top try-scorer, Wallaby wing David Campese. Now 32, the Canberra showman's extrovert playing style, trademark goosestep and love of running with the ball in hand have made him a legend in his own lifetime, and his name a byword for throwing caution to the four winds. He is one of rugby's great crowd-pleasers.

But while the sort of all-or-nothing game that Campese both preaches and practices wins him friends in the stands, it has landed him in hot water with team-mates from time to time – especially the hard men in the forwards who have little or no time for fancy concepts like "the expansive game".

A couple of high-profile errors have not helped Campese advance his cause among his large pack of detractors. Campese's problem is that he doesn't do things by half – his most famous blunder coming when he gifted the 1989 British Lions the try that effectively settled the deciding Test of the series. That momentary lapse brought a stinging rebuke from respected Australian commentator Gordon Bray: "That's Mickey Mouse rugby. You just should never do something like that when you're wearing the Green and Gold." In Australia, heroic defeat is not an option.

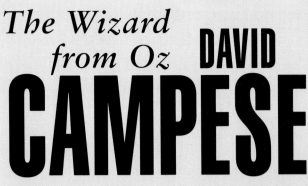

"*There's no point going to the grave without knowing what you can do. Once I get the ball, I am on my own.*"
DAVID CAMPESE

David Campese – the Wallaby wing is the ultimate crowd-pleaser.

Campese though is equally robust in his own defence. A spiky man off the pitch, he says that the game is all about enjoyment – for both players and fans – and that his instinctive flair has won more games than it has ever lost.

"My first responsibility is to myself," he says. "I want to satisfy myself by going out by going out there and doing something which you know no other player in the world has managed to pull off. The spectators are important, but only as a secondary consideration. I don't care if there are 70,000 or seven watching."

David Campese

BORN:	21 October 1962 Queanbeyan, Canberra
CLUBS:	Randwick and Mediolanum Milan
DEBUT:	vs. New Zealand, 1982
HEIGHT:	5ft 11in (1.82m)
WEIGHT:	13st 5lb (85kg)
JOB:	Sports shop owner

CAMPESE has played much of his club rugby in Italy over the past seven years. When in Europe, he plays for Milan and works as a PR executive for the club's sponsor – AC Milan soccer club owner, media magnate and political bigwig Silvio Berlusconi.

18

Rugby's first Millionaire

WILL CARLING

Will Carling – England's youngest and most successful captain.

It would be foolish to suppose that Will Carling, rugby superstar and a man who called himself "Rugby's first millionaire", has changed the game single-handedly in recent years, but there can be little doubt that the game's commercial and spectator appeal has grown massively since he first pulled on the England shirt as captain of his country back in 1988.

That game – in which England beat Australia 28–19 at Twickenham – ushered in an era of unprecedented stability and achievement by the national side. Used to being perpetual also-rans, England soon began to get a taste for success. Back-to-back Five Nations Championship Grand Slams in 1990 and 1991, as well as the hugely successful 1991 World Cup, saw interest in the game expand at breakneck pace.

By late 1991, Will Carling was the public face of rugby – the most recognisable rugby-playing Englishman since Bill Beaumont. But Carling wasn't just a pretty face, and his performances on the pitch were also a central part of England's success.

Carling is extremely strong, quick off the mark and has the ability to shrug off even the most committed tacklers. A run in 1990 at Twickenham, where he shrugged off Wales's Mark Titley twice as well as three other tacklers, personified Carling: quick, strong, brave, hard to pull down and with an eye for a gap.

Although Carling's form dropped off gradually as the Nineties progressed, he was still rock-like in defence, as good under fire as any player in world rugby. His early years as a fullback also meant that he had a cultured boot, giving a vital extra option in midfield. Questions remain, however, over his ability to vary tactics appropriately in his role as captain, while the feeling that England's attack relied too heavily on Jeremy Guscott was more than borne out during Guscott's enforced absence through injury.

> ❝*Will sets high standards. He puts pressure on himself. It's about finding a balance.*❞
>
> **GEOFF COOKE,** FORMER ENGLAND COACH

Will Carling

BORN:	12 December 1965 Bradford-Upon-Avon
CLUB:	Harlequins
DEBUT:	vs. France, 1988
HEIGHT:	5ft 11in (1.82m)
WEIGHT:	14st 2lb (90kg)
JOB:	Management trainer

CARLING *became England's youngest captain for 57 years when he was handed the reins aged 22 years 11 months, and is his country's most successful captain ever. Also England's most capped centre.*

Dead-Eye Diego DIEGO DOMINGUEZ

*Diego Dominguez –
a prolific place kicker.*

To most people, the term *Oriundi* will mean little. To Italy's Diego Dominguez, though, it meant plenty. Like uprooting himself from his native Argentina, moving 10,000 miles away to Milan in northern Italy, and being banned indefinitely from his own Union.

The term *Oriundi*, which applies to Dominguez, actually means an Italian born outside Italy. Under Italian law – which overrides any internal rugby regulations – anyone with an Italian parent or grandparent is de facto Italian and therefore able to come and work, live and play in Italy as if they were born there.

The upshot was that the cash-rich clubs of Italy went out and "acquired" players from the countries with the biggest Italian communities. Australia and South Africa were two, but by far the biggest source of players was Argentina. Because the Oriundi did not impinge upon the quota of foreigners in a side, Dominguez, then the understudy to the greatest Argentine fly-half ever, Hugo Porta, was just one of literally hundreds of players brought over to play for the top Italian clubs.

But signing with Milan back in the mid Eighties meant that Dominguez knew he would never be allowed to go back and play in, or for, Argentina. The true blue amateur Argentine Rugby Union were convinced that cash was involved and told every player who went that they would never play for Argentina again.

Faced with this prospect, Dominguez accepted the chance to play for Italy and has never looked back. He was superb in the last World Cup and has grown considerably in stature since then.

He was the architect of Italy's shock 1991 win over France and the near success in the two-Test tour to Australia, and has been consistently accurate with his place-kicking, scoring a world record eight penalties in Catania, Sicily, as Italy consigned an unfortunate Romania to the World Cup finals' toughest group.

> **"*Diego is the backbone of the Italian side.*"**
> **MARK ELLA,** ITALY'S COACH

Diego Dominguez

BORN:	25 April 1966 Cordoba, Argentina
CLUB:	Mediolanum Milan
DEBUT:	vs. France, 1991
HEIGHT:	5ft 8in (1.72m)
WEIGHT:	11st 8lb (72kg)
JOB:	Student

DOMINGUEZ *plays his club rugby at Mediolanum Milan, alongside the Aussie legend, winger David Campese.*

On a Wing and a Prayer
IEUAN EVANS

Ieuan Evans touches down against England (right) to seal a famous Five Nations victory at the National Stadium.

It is a testament to Ieuan Evans's try-scoring capabilities that, despite playing in some of the worst Welsh sides in living memory, in the summer of 1994 he became his country's top try-scorer. Evans – who scored two-thirds of Wales's try tally when he led them to the 1994 Five Nations Championship – notched up two successive hat-tricks as Wales obliterated an outclassed Spain and Portugal in World Cup qualifying matches by 54–0 and 102–11 respectively.

He is also Wales's longest-serving captain; the top try scorer in a full Test (four, against Canada in the 1987 World Cup) and in any match in a Welsh jersey (six, against Spain when playing for Wales B in 1985).

But, as ever with the truly great players, statistics can never tell the full story. Only by watching Evans in action, by seeing the silky smooth change of pace and the unerring choice to take on opponents on the outside – the real sign of confidence in a wing – is it possible to appreciate the genius of the man.

Strong in defence, Evans also has a superb sense of what options might be available. England fans, for instance, will remember the way in which Evans caught Rory Underwood napping to score the winning try for Wales at Cardiff in 1993. And there was another wonderful piece of mazy running and blistering pace that combined to produce a moment of virtuoso skill to spark a stirring fightback by the British Lions against when all seemed lost against the New Zealand Maoris.

Yet if Evans's strength is conjuring something out of nothing, his weakness has been a body which has let him down too often. Five dislocations and two operations marred his early career and meant that he missed the whole of the 1989–90 season, while further shoulder problems and a broken ankle in September 1994 were hardly the best preparations for the World Cup.

> **" He really is a sharp performer. He has pace and intelligence and could have graced most Welsh teams that I have seen. "**
>
> **PHIL BENNETT,**
> FORMER WELSH FLY-HALF

Ieuan Evans

BORN:	21 March 1964 Pontardulais
CLUB:	Llanelli
DEBUT:	vs. France, 1987
HEIGHT:	5ft 11in (1.80m)
WEIGHT:	13st 5lb (85kg)
JOB:	Leasing executive

EVANS *is a native Welsh-speaker, and he has commentated on rugby for the Welsh-language television channel.*

Samoan Man Mountain

PETER FATIALOFA

> " *Fats isn't a man of many words. He leads from the front and by example.* "
>
> **BRYAN WILLIAMS,**
> WESTERN SAMOA COACH

Peter Fatialofa – or "Fats" as he is known – has been the backbone of Western Samoa's rise to international prominence over the past five years. It has earned him a special place in the hearts of the tiny Pacific island nation whose people are besotted with the game.

Yet along with many of the other bulwarks of the 1991 Samoan side, Fatialofa's first priority for many years was to become an All Black. The former Auckland loosehead prop, though, counts it as one of his greatest strokes of luck that he failed to make the grade.

"My failed attempt to become an All Black was a blessing in disguise. I must have been destined to play for Western Samoa and help my nation fulfil its international aspirations," Fatialofa said. "In Britain people go to Oxford to further their education and give their career a meaning. We Samoans go to New Zealand to shape our rugby careers."

When Western Samoa decided to put in as strong a bid for World Cup honours as possible in 1991, manager Bryan Williams – himself a Samoan native who became a much-capped All Black wing – built his side around men like Fatialofa who had honed their skills overseas.

It was a policy that made sense. Along with New Zealand based forwards like Mark Birtwhistle, Matt Keenan, Pat Lam and Apollo Perelini, Fats helped Western Samoa construct a granite-hard pack well able to supply ample ball for their rampaging backs.

And of those who shone, Fatialofa was to the fore. An "old man" in the centre of a youthful pack, Fatialofa's experience was invaluable to the Samoans at the last World Cup. He became the focus for their virtually unstoppable rolling mauls and contributed an immense tightness in the loose, dragging the other seven Samoan forwards into a cohesive wedge. This Samoan is a man mountain indeed.

Peter Fatialofa hands off Argentina's overmatched Lisandro Arbizu during Western Samoa's 1991 35–12 World Cup victory.

Peter Fatialofa

BORN:	26 April 1959 Apia
CLUBS:	Manurewa and Counties (NZ)
DEBUT:	vs. Fiji, 1990
HEIGHT:	6ft (1.84m)
WEIGHT:	18st 2lbs (115kg)
JOB:	Piano mover

FATIALOFA *decided to join the Samoan cause when his father – an Apia postmaster – died shortly before the 1991 World Cup.*

All Black to Front

SEAN FITZPATRICK

Sean Fitzpatrick – the most capped All Black hooker of all time.

When New Zealand triumphed in the first World Cup back in 1987, much of their success was built on a pack which steamrollered the opposition. As Australian lock Peter FitzSimons recalled after meeting much the same pack three years later: "I looked up from the bottom of a ruck and it looked like a Multi-Addidassed centipede passing overhead."

And if the All Blacks' irresistible campaign to win the inaugural William Webb Ellis Trophy was illuminated by brilliant play from the backs, especially John Kirwan and John Gallagher, it was based on a forward dynamism unequalled before or since. In 1987 the core of that effort was a rock-solid front row which eventually became Loe–Fitzpatrick–McDowell – a combination which has passed into legend.

Mobile and gritty, Sean Fitzpatrick, the All Black skipper has provided the rest of the rugby world with the prototype player on which the new breed of young hookers have modelled themselves. Generally reckoned to be the best lineout thrower in world rugby these days, Fitzpatrick also has a bull-like strength that makes him a good scrummager.

But it is his immense speed, good hands and his ability to pop up as the first man in support that has marked him out a world class player. There are few hookers who have scored seven tries in a career spanning almost a decade of top level rugby.

Softly-spoken and quiet off the pitch, Fitzpatrick is a notorious "sledger" on the field. He was the victim of an infamous incident when South African prop Johan Le Roux took a bite out of his ear during the 1994 Second Test at Athletic Park in Wellington.

Since the last World Cup, Fitzpatrick has helped New Zealand to their first series win in South Africa and seen off the British Lions. And now, despite the challenge of "Stormin'" Norm Hewett, he is set to become the most-capped All Black of all time.

Sean Fitzpatrick

BORN:	4 June 1963 Auckland
CLUBS:	University and Auckland
DEBUT:	vs. France, 1986
HEIGHT:	6ft (1.83m)
WEIGHT:	14st 10lb (93kg)
JOB:	Marketing promotions officer

FITZPATRICK hasn't missed a New Zealand Test match since he wrested the No.2 shirt from Hika Reid in 1986 – a run of 56 consecutive matches.

> **"** His power, allied to his absolute relish for the physical confrontations and almost provocatively competitive approach, have made him one of the key players of his generation. **"**
>
> **JOHN HART,**
> FORMER AUCKLAND AND NEW ZEALAND COACH

Bambi on Benzedrine SIMON
GEOGHEGAN

Simon Geoghegan, showman extra-ordinaire, is the nearest thing to perpetual motion you will ever see on a rugby pitch. There's none of the "stand on the wing and wait for the ball to come my way" about Geoghegan. He's all action, looking to get his hands on the ball at every opportunity.

So manic is the way the Bath winger bobs about that more than one coach has expressed a concern over whether or not he would pass the post-match drugs test. That doubt accounts for his nickname of "Bambi" – someone once described him as "Bambi on Benzedrine" and it just stuck!

It's not too difficult to see why Geoghegan figures so highly in Irish minds. Despite receiving just two passes in open play during the 1994 Five Nations, the outstanding moment of the tournament for the Irish was the sight of Geoghegan scorching around England wing Tony Underwood for the game's only try. That match-winning effort was classic Geoghegan: sassy, unexpected and totally audacious.

If there's one thing you can say about Geoghegan, it's that his ebullient personality is completely reflected in the way he plays rugby. He has supreme confidence in his own abilities and it shows.

Yet Geoghegan also expects a lot of others, and gets extremely frustrated when those around him do not measure up to his expectations. He got himself in hot water with his former club London Irish and with Ireland when he criticised the coaching structures and was summarily dropped from both sides.

But if Geoghegan can be difficult, according to former London Irish and Connacht coach George Hooks, that is part of the make-up that makes him such an outstanding player.

"When you take on Simon Geoghegan," said Hooks, "you take on extra baggage. And when you take on that baggage, you've got to appreciate that there's a very narrow line between genius and madness."

> "I think he is one of the outstanding international wingers in the world."
>
> **GEORGE HOOKS,**
> FORMER CONNACHT COACH

Simon Geoghegan – the wing proves there is a fine line between genius and madness.

Simon Geoghegan

BORN:	1 September 1968 Barnet, Hertfordshire
CLUB:	Bath
DEBUT:	vs. France, 1991
HEIGHT:	6ft (1.83m)
WEIGHT:	13st 2lb (84kg)
JOB:	Solicitor

GEOGHEGAN *was actually born in England, but to Irish parents. "I was brought up in England, but we've got a very close-knit family and I've always considered myself Irish," he explained.*

The Rapier's Thrust

JEREMY GUSCOTT

There is a time and a place for every player to burst on to the international scene, but few have done it with quite the same degree of high impact as England centre Jeremy Guscott. With only a single cap against Romania to his name – albeit a debut that yielded three tries – Guscott was pulled into the British Lions by coach Ian McGeechan, a fan of the elusive Bath player. It was a decision which bore spectacular fruit in the Second Test against the Wallabies in 1989.

The game was still too tight to call – the Lions clinging on to a narrow lead – when Guscott was called on as a substitute for the injured Scott Hastings and immediately made his mark. Receiving the ball in mid-stride on the Australian 22-metre-line, Guscott barely checked as he dropped the ball on to his right foot, poked through a cheeky grubber kick and fell on the ball over the line.

It was a moment of inspired brilliance which won the series and typified the way in which the young Bath man was to set the game alight. Guscott is a Bath boy through and through, and has played for the West Country club since his days in the mini section.

Guscott is as close to a living rugby legend as it is possible to get. He has it all – and plenty of it: he can kick, he can step on the gas and accelerate into space like no other player in the world.

His centre partnership with Will Carling has been the backbone of England's Five Nations and World Cup challenges for the past six years and will prove to be so again in South Africa. Carling provides the bustling crash ball threat while Guscott is the silky assassin capable of ripping badly aligned defences to shreds. It is the bludgeon and the rapier … and it works.

Jeremy Guscott – returned to international action in 1994 after injury.

"*The most phenomenal tackling centre I have ever seen.*"

RAY SOUTHAM,
CANTERBURY DIRECTOR OF RUGBY, SPEAKING AFTER SEEING THE 1993 BRITISH LIONS DEFEAT HIS TEAM

Jeremy Guscott

BORN:	7 July 1965 Bath
CLUB:	Bath
DEBUT:	vs. Romania, 1989
HEIGHT:	6ft 1in (1.85m)
WEIGHT:	13st 6lb (86kg)
JOB:	PR executive

GUSCOTT *is also a keen golfer and, despite only starting the game at the age of 26, now has a handicap of eight.*

Stormin' Norman NORM HADLEY

The first thing that strikes you about Norm Hadley is his sheer size. When Hadley was about to appear in an advertisement for an outsize men's retailer in London, he was amazed to find that he was only halfway up their size range! But he is huge. At 6ft 7in, and weighing in at somewhere between 18 and 24 stone, Stormin' Norm is by far the biggest man in Test rugby today.

> **"** *I'm probably one of the worst line-out jumpers in the world. You couldn't swish a blade of grass under my boots when I go up. But I am physical. I get my own ball and the opposition don't like it.* **"**
>
> **NORM HADLEY**

And it was that bulk which comprised the heart of Canada's amazing effort in the 1991 World Cup. Nowhere was Hadley more in evidence than against New Zealand in the quarter-final in Lille.

In torrential rain, Hadley and his cohorts drove the All Blacks back time and time again, beating the New Zealanders at their own game – not what you would exactly call an everyday event. Although the Canadians eventually lost the tie, their pack had proved it could live with the best, and Hadley was the pick of the Canuck eight.

It was that performance in particular, as well as his line-out ability when jumping at number four, which earned Hadley his place in the Ultimate World XV second row alongside Wade Dooley after that tournament.

At the time Hadley played for the University of British Columbia Old Boys and used the exposure to get in a bit of travelling. He joined Suntory in Japan, but the Land of the Rising Sun wasn't quite ready for a man as big or as outgoing as Hadley and he went to play for Wasps in England.

Sadly, a broken leg in 1993–94 kept him out of action for the best part of a year. On the pro side, though, Hadley now has less problems containing a fiery temper which occasionally threatened to get him in serious trouble.

Norm Hadley – the biggest man in international rugby.

Norm Hadley

BORN:	10 October 1962 Vancouver
CLUBS:	UBCOB and Wasps
DEBUT:	vs. Tonga, 1987
HEIGHT:	6ft 7in (2.01m)
WEIGHT:	21st 2lb (120kg)
JOB:	Fund manager

IN NOVEMBER 1994, *Hadley made the front page of* The Times *in England after he sorted out two drunken thugs who were terrorising early-morning commuters. They hadn't realised quite how big he was until he got up and pushed one of them. The two fled at the next station.*

Captain Courageous GAVIN HASTINGS

Gavin Hastings is a man of few words who leads by example. As the mainstay of the great Scottish side of the mid Eighties, Hastings and his brother Scott are the last remnants of a side which included players like David Sole, Finlay Calder, John Jeffrey and Gary Armstrong.

But if Hastings appears a bit laid back at times, he gives occasional glimpses of what it means to him to wear the Scottish jersey. For instance, after Scotland's narrow 1994 Five Nations defeat by England, Hastings, called in to talk to the television cameras, could not hide his bitter disappointment and, as tears welled up in his eyes, he was forced to abandon the interview.

Such a powerful motivator is the quietly-spoken Hastings, who is happy to let his play do his talking, that he, rather than Will Carling, was chosen to lead the British Lions' 1993 tour to New Zealand. And leading from the front, Hastings confirmed his position as a supreme captain.

But Hastings is also the best fullback in the world. A rock under the high ball and a sledgehammer tackler, he likes to burst into the back line to break through opposition defences in battering-ram style charges.

He developed into one of the best place-kickers in Britain, and was the first British player to score 500 international points in a landmark 1993–4 season which also saw him earn his 50th cap.

Although capable of knocking over some absolutely huge penalty kicks, Hastings has a strange habit of being wayward with kicks from directly in front of the posts. Hence one of his main regrets in life is the kick he missed from that position against England in the 1991 World Cup semi-final. It was that kick that allowed England to win by 9–6 and Hastings has never forgiven himself.

*Gavin Hastings –
a defensive bulwark.*

"*Gavin is central to everything we do.*"

IAN McGEECHAN,
FORMER SCOTLAND COACH

Gavin Hastings

BORN:	3 January 1962 Edinburgh
CLUB:	Watsonians
DEBUT:	vs. France, 1986
HEIGHT:	6ft 2in (1.90m)
WEIGHT:	14st 11lb (94kg)
JOB:	Sports marketing executive

YOUNGER *brother Scott has shadowed Gavin's international career. As well as both playing for Watsonians, Scotland and the British Lions together, the two brothers also won their 50th caps in the 1994 Five Nations home defeat to France.*

Wales's Mr Reliable NEIL JENKINS

In 1994, goal-kicker Neil Jenkins overtook former captain Paul Thorburn as his country's record points scorer and he became Wales's most important player. Throughout Wales's World Cup qualification games, it was the quiet, modest Jenkins whose unerring eye for goal saw Wales through. While he picked up huge hauls against Spain and Portugal in the preliminary qualifiers, it was against the aspiring powers of Romania and Italy that Jenkins's input was absolutely vital.

> **"My kicking used to be a bit erratic, but now I've been taught to visualise the ball as it flies through the posts. The results of that coaching speak for themselves."**
>
> NEIL JENKINS

In Bucharest, it was only Jenkins's accuracy that kept Wales in touch with a surprisingly robust Romanian side. With the home forwards dominating the Welsh, especially at the lineout, the visitors won almost no possession throughout the game and had to rely on the Pontypridd fly-half. But Jenkins's aim was again flawless, helping Wales to a 16–7 win. At the crucial time, it was to Jenkins Wales turned, and Mr Reliable didn't let them down.

He was similarly impressive in the close win over Italy at the National Stadium in Cardiff. Billed as a kicking duel between Jenkins and Diego Dominguez, the little Italian fly-half came off second best as Jenkins pumped kicks over from almost every distance and angle. The eventual winning margin of 29–19 was a direct reflection of how that kicking contest eventually went.

And if Wales are to progress in South Africa, they will need Jenkins to show that sort of form again. With the era of the Pontypool front row and "Merv The Swerve" long gone, it has been a while since Wales have had a pack which could dominate as completely as they did in the Seventies.

But that does not necessarily equal defeat when you have a kicker of Jenkins's calibre waiting to punish indiscretions from anywhere in the opposition half.

Neil Jenkins – at present probably the best goal kicker in rugby.

Neil Jenkins

BORN:	8 July 1971 Church Village, Pontypridd
CLUB:	Pontypridd
DEBUT:	vs. England, 1991
HEIGHT:	5ft 10in (1.78m)
WEIGHT:	13st 7lb (81kg)
JOB:	Car hire firm PR Consultant

JENKINS is the top points scorer in Welsh rugby. He overtook Paul Thorburn and also held the world record for penalties in a game, striking eight in the 24–26 loss to Canada in November 1993.

The Italian Job MICHAEL LYNAGH

Michael Lynagh – the best all-round player in the world.

There cannot be many harder acts to follow than Mark Ella, one of the greatest fly-halves ever to play for Australia, but nobody could have done a better job than current Wallaby captain Michael Lynagh. Ella's presence meant that Lynagh was forced to play at centre. But even there "Noddy" – as Lynagh is known – impressed immensely, and he was an integral member of the 1984 Grand Slam tour of Britain.

L ynagh, a virtually infallible place kicker, has since gone on to amass a world record of over 800 points – a tally which only New Zealand's legendary Grant Fox ever came close to emulating.

Yet while the rest of Fox's game didn't match up to his phenomenal kicking ability, the ability to rack up points with his boot is far from the only weapon in Lynagh's armoury. An accomplished distributor of the ball, Lynagh is also a proponent of the running game, and more than capable of speeding through any gap opponents are unwise enough to leave.

He has demonstrated this flair on countless occasions at events like the Hong Kong Sevens and in the Italian League where he spends his summers, yet his commitment to risk received its sternest test in the 1991 World Cup. Entering the last minutes, and down 18–13 in the quarter-final against Ireland in Dublin, Lynagh received the ball on the Irish 22. What should he do – go for the drop goal and hope to get another chance or go for broke? Lynagh passed to Jason Little, looped around to take the return, and then slipped the tackle to go over for the decisive try which stunned 50,000 Irishmen ready to celebrate a famous victory.

That run, which typified the Lynagh approach, sent the Wallabies on their way to winning the Webb Ellis Trophy.

> **"** *Michael masterminds it all, dominating the tactical battles and controlling the flow of games beautifully. He is such a great player – as good as I've ever seen.* **"**
>
> **MARK ELLA,**
> FORMER AUSTRALIAN FLY-HALF

Michael Lynagh

BORN:	25 October 1963 Brisbane
CLUBS:	Queensland University and Benetton Treviso
DEBUT:	vs. Fiji, 1984
HEIGHT:	5ft 10in (1.78m)
WEIGHT:	12st 9lb (80kg)
JOB:	Commercial real estate manager

LYNAGH *puts his goal-kicking accuracy down to the work he does on mental approach and preparation with his father Ian, a noted sports psychologist.*

AUSTRALIA

POSITION: FLY-HALF

29

Pugilistic Puma Prop FEDERICO MENDEZ

It was about halfway through a comfortable England victory over Argentina at Twickenham in 1990 when Federico Mendez, just 18 back then, took exception to a bit of over zealous footwork and burst onto the international scene – for all the wrong reasons.

Intent on taking matters into his own hands, the next time a bit of pushing and shoving occurred, he just launched himself at the nearest man in an England shirt. That man was Paul Ackford, who was looking the other way at the time. Poor old Ackers never stood a chance; his next memory was waking up in the tunnel to see the now sent off Mendez following him.

England won that game 51–0 – ample retribution for their 15–13 defeat in Buenos Aires earlier in the year –

Federico Mendez	
BORN:	19 August 1972 Rosario
CLUB:	Rosario
DEBUT:	vs. England, 1990
HEIGHT:	6ft 2in (1.88m)
WEIGHT:	17st 12lb (109kg)
JOB:	Student

ARGENTINA *have been experimenting with Mendez at hooker, where they feel he may be free to play an even greater part in loose play and he may well appear there during the World Cup.*

but the abiding memory of the encounter will be the sheer raw power of that 18-year-old prop.

Mendez is a physical monster. At over 6ft and approaching 18 stone, he is a huge hulk of a man with a strength that is well in advance of his relatively young age for a prop, most of whom reach their peak around 31.

Mendez is a country boy from upstate Rosario, possibly the most world's most forbidding destination for touring sides. They're a passionate lot where Mendez comes from, and touring sides have had to be protected by the army – England saw their flag burnt in the stands just as they were about to kick off.

It is a measure of the player that, in a country where ferocious front row forwards are plentiful, Mendez still reigns king. He only got his chance when the former incumbent, Serafin Dengra, was lured to Italy for the lira and was summarily excommunicated by the Argentine union.

But Mendez doesn't care – he's got what he has always perceived to be his birthright.

> **"He packs one hell of a punch."**
>
> **PAUL ACKFORD,**
> FORMER ENGLAND
> SECOND ROW FORWARD

Federico Mendez – a front row forward of immense raw power.

A Centre of Excellence PIETER MULLER

When South Africa finally came back into international competition, they had been away so long that they had doubts about all of their players. Would they be able to adapt to the pace of the game at international level? Would they be able to adjust to the different law interpretations? And, most importantly, would they be good enough.

But if there was one player over whom there were never any question marks, it was precocious young Natal centre Pieter Muller.

Still only 22 when South Africa took on the All Blacks in the pressure-cooker atmosphere of Ellis Park, Muller came through with flying colours despite being on a side that lost 27–24, an emphatic win which only looked respectable because of two late Springbok tries by Danie Gerber.

Muller had signed a declaration of intent that day. Although the team didn't play well, Muller did, picking up a try on his debut. Such was Muller's influence that he was the only Springbok to have played every Test since re-entry to international competition in 1992 to the start of the 1994–95 Northern Hemisphere season, and that despite there being a glut of top class centres pushing for the spot.

> "He is the one South African player who we all knew for sure would make the grade."
>
> **JOHN ROBBIE,** FORMER BRITISH LIONS SCRUM-HALF

An abrasive, hard-tackling and hard-running back who relies on sheer power allied to a sharp turn of pace, the 6ft 3in Muller is one of the bigger specimens inhabiting Test threequarter lines. Yet if he a has one weakness – other than that he has a suspect temperament – it is that Muller's attacking ploys are not subtle. He is a crash ball merchant through and through, and even if it is a ploy that is well suited by the hard grounds of the High Veldt, it may not prove as effective as sheer speed undoubtedly will during the coming tournament.

Pieter Muller

BORN:	5 May 1969 Bloemfontein
CLUBS:	College Rovers and Natal
DEBUT:	vs. New Zealand, 1992
HEIGHT:	6ft 3in (1.90m)
WEIGHT:	14st 2lb (90kg)
JOB:	Sales Executive

PIETER'S elder brother, Helgard, also started life playing for the Orange Free State, and collected two caps – against the Cavaliers in 1986 and against the Rest of the World in 1989.

SOUTH AFRICA

POSITION: CENTRE

The Tongan Torpedo

WILLIE OFAHENGAUE

Above: Willie Ofahengaue takes on the Irish defence during the 1991 World Cup quarter-final.

"*He's not too bad for someone who wanted to be an All Black, is he?*"

BOB DWYER,
AUSTRALIAN COACH

The strangest thing about Viliame Ofahengaue – aka "Willie-O" or "The Tongan Torpedo" – is that he ever ended up playing for Australia. But it a strange sequence of events for which the Wallabies will always be eternally grateful.

A Tongan by birth, Ofahengaue had his first big break when he moved to New Zealand to live. He brought with him the South Seas island trait of bone-jarring tackling, but combined it with an ability to consistently make ground with the ball in hand. Tacklers just bounced off him.

He was drafted into the 1988 New Zealand Schools party to tour Australia, and was its outstanding player. But, Ofahengaue found his immigration papers were not in order and he was denied re-entry at Auckland airport.

Desperate, Ofahengaue went to live with an uncle in Australia as a temporary measure. Taking advantage of Ofahengaue's new address, the Australian Rugby Union petitioned on his behalf and, two years later, he was playing for Australia – against New Zealand in the Bledisloe Cup.

Ofahengaue's importance to the Wallabies cannot be underestimated. In 1991, he was the catalyst for the development of an outstanding young pack, acting as the link man between the halfback pairing of Nick Farr-Jones and Michael Lynagh and the forwards who were brilliant in tight and loose.

A troublesome knee injury limited his effectiveness after 1991, but his form in the summer of 1994, particularly helping Australia to regain the Bledisloe Cup, suggested that he was back to his best.

A painfully shy family man and devoted Christian, there is a very good chance that Ofahengaue would be playing rugby league by now had he not suffered from an injury doubt. It has taken a supreme effort by the ARU to keep him from signing for the Newcastle Knights and South Queensland Crushers.

Willie Ofahengaue

BORN:	3 May 1968 Tonga
CLUBS:	Manly and NSW
DEBUT:	vs. New Zealand, 1990
HEIGHT:	6ft 4in (1.93m)
WEIGHT:	16st 7lb (105kg)
JOB:	Pile Driver

THE *most difficult moment of Ofahengaue's working life was when he turned up at work the Monday after helping New South Wales to a record 71–8 win over the Welsh tourists in 1991 – his boss is a Welshman!*

Mr Squeaky Clean FRANCOIS PIENAAR

South African captain Francois Pienaar is a nice guy – I mean a really nice guy. A great PR man for his team and country, he has a problem in that this doesn't necessarily make for a good rugby player, and while he is a superb ambassador for the South African game, many have questioned his on-field ability.

Predictably enough, few of those doubters come from outside South Africa or from Pienaar's province, Transvaal. But such is the nature of domestic rugby politics in the Republic that there is never a genuine consensus on the composition of the national side, and those who owe their allegiance to Northern Transvaal and Western Province, in particular, have found the appointment of a player from Louis Luyt's Transvaal hard to stomach.

Pienaar has borne the innuendo and charges of jobs for the boys with fortitude. In fact, the 6ft 4in flanker has gradually warmed to the task of captaining the Springboks, and carried out the task with distinction on the late 1994 tour of Wales, Scotland and Ireland.

A barnstorming flanker himself, Pienaar has gradually managed to coax the best out of the South African forwards, the side's weak point over the past three years.

Pienaar started off his international career against France, and hardly got off to a flier. Having drawn the First Test in Durban 20–20, South Africa lost the Second at Transvaal's home stadium of Ellis Park by 18–17 – their first home series defeat by France.

Pienaar had made his Test debut in the same game as he had become

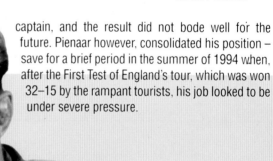

Francois Pienaar	
BORN:	2 January 1967 Johannesburg
CLUB:	Transvaal
DEBUT:	vs. France, 1993
HEIGHT:	6ft 4in (1.92m)
WEIGHT:	17st 10lb (104kg)
JOB:	PR executive

PIENAAR also captained Transvaal to a Currie Cup and Super Ten double in 1993, and retained the 1994 Currie Cup.

> **"The South African captain has been a beacon of sanity for the Springboks."**
> **RUGBY NEWS**

captain, and the result did not bode well for the future. Pienaar however, consolidated his position – save for a brief period in the summer of 1994 when, after the First Test of England's tour, which was won 32–15 by the rampant tourists, his job looked to be under severe pressure.

Francois Pienaar – a driving force on the flank for South Africa.

> *"As mobile as a barge and about as likely to run with the ball in hand as the QEII, Rees is nevertheless the best distributor playing in Britain."*
>
> **THE SUNDAY TIMES**

The Siege Gun GARETH REES

Few people would describe Canada's style as expansive. No, their's is a British style which revolves around eight huge men grappling for the ball, which is passed out by the scrum-half and then kicked by the fly-half for the grunts to go downfield in a trial of strength.

Ten-man rugby is the Canadian hallmark, but the single most important man in the equation is not numbered between one and nine, it's number 10 – the fly-half. And Canada's fly-half is Gareth Rees. He is by far the most experienced player in their squad and it is his huge touch-finders and booming up-and-unders that have allowed Canada to profit prodigiously from the pack's graft.

Rees, whose precocious talent had already been recognised back home – especially by his rugby-mad, Welsh-born, father – began his rugby education in earnest in London under the tutelage of Harrow School's coach Roger Uttley in 1985.

To say Rees was a success would be a vast understatement. Within a year of arriving in England – and still at school – he was playing at Twickenham as his club Wasps met Bath in the national Cup final. Although Wasps lost 25–17 to Bath, Rees was clearly a star in the making.

And if the chunky Canadian was never going to be an integral part of the running game himself, he still had the sense to know when to ship the ball on and when to hold it up. Then there are those up-and-unders! Rees has a mountainous, spiralling, hanging kick which terrorises opposing full-backs.

Rees is of greater benefit to team-mates in that he knows Five Nations rugby inside out. For a group of players from, in rugby terms, a remote country who, inevitably, have trouble in keeping tabs on who's who in the outside world, Rees's experience with Merignac in France and now Newport in Wales has proved a source of vital information.

Gareth Rees – the mastermind behind the rise and rise of Canada.

Gareth Rees

BORN:	30 June 1967 Vancouver
CLUBS:	Newport & Oxford University
DEBUT:	vs. Tonga, 1987
HEIGHT:	5ft 11in (1.81m)
WEIGHT:	13st 9lb (92kg)
JOB:	Student

REES kicked the winning, injury-time conversion when Canada shocked Wales 26–24 at Cardiff in 1993.

Olivier Roumat

BORN:	16 June 1966 Mont de Marsan
CLUB:	Dax
DEBUT:	vs. New Zealand, 1989
HEIGHT:	6ft 7in (2.01m)
WEIGHT:	17st 5lb (111kg)
JOB:	Surveyor

THE *only time Roumat has been sent off was during the biggest match of his life – for the World XV against New Zealand in 1992.*

Scaling the Heights OLIVIER
ROUMAT

Teenage basketball prodigy Olivier Roumat didn't even pick up a rugby ball in anger until he was almost 18 years of age, virtually a pensioner in hard school of French rugby. Yet by the age of 23, Roumat was enjoying life in the engine room of the second row against those most formidable of opponents, New Zealand.

The 6ft 7in giant's exclusion from the game wasn't his decision, but his father's. Ferdinand Roumat was a useful number 8 who turned out for Mont de Marsan in the French Championship final of 1959 against Racing Club de Paris. Ferdinand had himself come late to the game, not having played until he was 20, but he had seen many of the young players he started off with fall by the wayside.

Once started, though, there was little stopping the athletic Olivier. Although he was forced to move to Dax from his home town club of Mont de Marsan, after a row with the management, the Daxois took him in and Roumat prospered at the famous club.

Although an outstanding line-out jumper, Roumat had always been a number 8 and didn't move to the second row until French coach Jacques Fouroux – who was then experimenting with playing five number 8s in the scrum – suggested to the young Roumat that that was where his future lay.

Although Roumat suffered from being shunted from second row to number 8 as his club did its best to accommodate both him and the national number 8 of the day, Laurent Rodriguez, his talent was sufficiently precocious for him to establish himself and he has gone on to be the mainstay of France's forward effort. In the summer of 1993, Roumat captained his country to their first series win over South Africa since 1958.

Olivier Roumat's line-out presence is vital to France.

"*We play too much rugby in France and I look around and see so many precocious talents that burn out early because they started too early.*"

OLIVIER ROUMAT,
ON RUGBY'S PHYSICAL DEMANDS

> *"Philippe has the strength of a bull but the touch of a piano player."*
>
> **JACQUES FOUROUX,**
> FORMER FRENCH COACH

Sella's Swansong
PHILIPPE SELLA

France's Philippe Sella is the most capped player in the history of the game. In fact, he is the only player in the game's history to have passed the 100 cap mark. The Agen centre first turned out for France in a full international as long ago as 1982, when he made his debut in his country's surprise 13–9 loss to Romania in Bucharest, having already represented France at Schools, Junior and Student levels.

D espite this inauspicious debut, Sella's hard-hitting play in midfield caught the selectors' attention and earned him a place in the side that lined up to play Argentina. He became a regular fixture in French teams during the mid Eighties, playing in 45 consecutive Tests until injury intervened in 1987.

Sella's contribution has been felt most strongly in defence. His spectacular ability to drive the ball-carrier back in the tackle has made him a favourite with the "Big Hits" video compilers, although he has also made contributions to several bits of video evidence at disciplinary tribunals as well.

The most notable instance of this was on 1994's tour of Canada, when Sella was sent off for punching in the ill-tempered 18–16 shock defeat at the hands of Canada at Fletcher's Field in Ontario. But he is not a dirty player – just extremely uncompromising. And, like all great players, Sella is not just a defensive strongman. His average of one try every four international games is one of the best in world rugby.

Although the 1994 World Cup is sure to be his swansong, Sella, who played in the most memorable World Cup match ever played – against Australia in the 1987 semi-final – the former French captain, now 33, has enjoyed an Indian summer. His Test career looked to be over when he and the rest of the "Old Guard" were dropped after the disastrous 24–20 defeat by Argentina in Nantes, the first time the Pumas had ever won in France.

Philippe Sella

BORN:	14 February 1962 Clairac
CLUB:	Agen
DEBUT:	vs. Romania, 1982
HEIGHT:	5ft 11in (1.80m)
WEIGHT:	13st 4lb (84kg)
JOB:	Businessman

SELLA scored a try in every match during the 1986 Five Nations Championship, a feat accomplished by only three other men.

Philippe Sella is one of the formidable defenders in the game.

> "*Wood is superb. He is a world-class player.*"
>
> **BOB DWYER,**
> AUSTRALIAN COACH

Ireland's Worst Kept Secret KEITH
WOOD

It began as a rumour some two years ago. There is this kid in Limerick, see, and he can't get into the provincial side because Ireland hooker Terry Kingston is blocking his way. But he's brilliant.

A nd so it proved. He knew it would take a while, but uncompromising Garryowen hooker Keith Wood was sure he'd make it. What he cannot have foreseen is quite how spectacularly he did. Going on Ireland's 1994 summer tour to Australia as part of a young party, following a spate of withdrawals, Wood was one of the raw recruits who rose to

Keith Wood has gone from nowhere to being touted as one of the world's best within the space of a season.

the challenge. And boy did he rise to the challenge.

Wood was irresistible on that tour and simply grabbed hold of the Test number 2 jersey with an almost literal and figurative "That's mine!" And in the Tests, even playing in a mediocre side that was well beaten, he was a revelation.

His work-rate in tight and loose was staggering, and if anyone doubted that the hooker was not the real thing, they should have heard Australian coach Bob Dwyer sing his praises. "World class" and "outstanding" are not comments that trip off Dwyer's tongue easily; in this case they recognized that Wood had completely outplayed Phil Kearns – rated by many as the best hooker in the world – in both Tests.

His presence galvanises sides like no other forward in recent times. Even at club level, he screams out for the ball, gets it and drags his team-mates along with him, willing or no.

Hooking between Nick Popplewell and Peter Clohessy, Wood is one third of a front row as good as any in world rugby. It is that base around which Ireland need to build their World Cup challenge, and if Wood can keep his temper and inclination to mete out summary justice in check, then he will have a prime role in that campaign.

KEITH WOOD

BORN:	27 January 1972 Limerick
CLUB:	Garryowen
DEBUT:	vs. Australia, 1994
HEIGHT:	6ft (1.83m)
WEIGHT:	15st 12lb (101kg)
JOB:	Bank Official

WOOD'S father, Gordon, also played for Ireland 29 times (1954–61) and also made two Test appearances for the British Lions side that toured New Zealand in 1959.

CHAPTER 3

The Qualifying COUNTRIES

Rugby has long been dominated by the "Big Eight", where the game has its deepest roots and its widest following. But outside the narrow confines of the Five Nations – England, France, Ireland, Scotland and Wales – plus Australia, New Zealand and South Africa, there have always been many countries where rugby was fostered by a committed few. Prior to the advent of the World Cup, their heroic feats were almost unnoticed.

So close – the USA Eagles lost narrowly to the Argentine Pumas in Buenos Aires and so were knocked out of the qualifying competition for the 1995 finals.

The Rugby World Cup has revolutionised the global game. The tournament has provided a wealth of opportunity for the nations which were often overlooked by the traditional powers in the game. Where the likes of Italy and Canada were awarded only fixtures against second-string sides, World Cup games are full international fixtures where the Big Eight put out a top side. That resulted in painful losses – such as Italy's 70–6 drubbing by New Zealand in 1987 – yet it has also given Canada and Western Samoa the chance to join the game's elite.

THE QUALIFYING GROUPS

It is that potential to go to the finals and compete on equal terms with the best in the world that makes the qualifying rounds so frantic and interesting. And none more so this time around than in the African Zone, where the Ivory Coast surprised everyone by overcoming much-fancied Namibia en route to a place in the last 16. Almost everyone had expected Namibia to go through from the African Zone. Yet in a stunning week at Casablanca, the North African champions overcame Southern Africa's champs, 13–12, in one of the most intense qualifying games the competition has ever seen. When hosts Morocco – who beat the Ivory Coast earlier in the competition – drew with Namibia in the final game, the men from the Gulf of Guinea knew they had booked their place in South Africa.

If the Ivory Coast were the surprise package of the African section, then Japan's triumph was at least a return to the status quo in the Asian Zone. Yet despite the same outcome as in 1990, the Kuala Lumpur (Malaysia) leg of the qualifiers was every bit as exciting as anything served up in West Africa, mainly because of the renewal of hostilities between perennial regional rivals Japan and South Korea. The Koreans – who so nearly beat Japan to qualify for the last World Cup – were edged out by 26–11 in the tournament final, but only after some spectacular pyrotechnics in the earlier rounds.

RECORD SCORE

One of the big talking points of the competition was Hong Kong's 164–13 win over a hapless Singapore side, a loss which brought their points conceded tally to 323 in three games. The competition exploded when Japan played Taiwan. A Japanese high tackle saw all 15 Taiwan players and the five replacements rush off the bench to protest, after which a ten-minute full-scale brawl broke out.

Western Samoa's qualification as quarter-finalists from the 1991 tournament meant that Fiji and Tonga were left to fight it out for the qualifying place from the Pacific Zone. In two typically brutal contests, both sides won away from home. Fiji lost out after Tonga's 13-point win in Suva gave them a virtually unassailable lead. Fiji did well to travel to Nuku'alofa and win 15–10, but it was not enough, while Tonga make their way to Pretoria.

As with the Pacific Zone, the Americas Group was guaranteed to see a former qualifier eliminated. Because Canada qualified as quarter-finalists from 1991, the USA and Argentina were left to compete for the one qualifying place. With the Eagles getting steadily more competitive under new coach Jack Clarke, the result was far from a walkover, but the Pumas' heavy schedule had prepared them better for the home and away series, which they won 28–22 and 16–11.

The European Zone was split into three sections (West, Central and East) and there was little doubt about which countries would come through. Wales, Italy and Romania respectively qualified, notching up some massive scores on the way – Wales defeated Portugal 102–11, Italy won 104–8 over the Czech Republic, and Romania mauled Germany 60–3 – representing each side's most emphatic victory. Wales then beat Romania and Italy to qualify as Europe 1, while Italy's victory over Romania ranked them as Europe 2, and consigned Romania to the dreaded Europe 3 status and a place in the "Group of Death".

QUALIFYING RESULTS

EUROPEAN ZONE WEST
Preliminaries: Denmark 0, Andorra 3; Denmark 8, Switzerland 3; Switzerland 14, Andorra 0 (*winner*: Switzerland). **Round-robin**: Spain 40, Switzerland 0; Belgium 3, Portugal 8; Belgium 3, Spain 67; Portugal 32, Switzerland 0; Switzerland 3, Belgium 42; Portugal 15, Spain 37 (*winner*: Spain; *runner-up*: Portugal). **Play-offs**: Portugal 11, Wales 102; Spain 0, Wales 54; Spain 35, Portugal 19 (*winner*: Wales).

EUROPEAN ZONE CENTRAL
Preliminary: Hungary 8, Israel 67. **Round-robin**: Israel 10, Sweden 26; Czech Republic 6, The Netherlands 42; The Netherlands 56, Israel 0; Czech Republic 34, Sweden 7; The Netherlands 31, Sweden 6; Czech Republic 28, Israel 0 (*winner*: The Netherlands; *runner-up*: Czech Republic). **Play-offs**: The Netherlands 33, Czech Republic 9; Italy 104, Czech Republic 8; Italy 63, The Netherlands 9 (*winner*: Italy).

EUROPEAN ZONE EAST
Preliminaries 1: Germany 31, Lithuania 5; Latvia 5, Germany 27; Lithuania 6, Latvia 7 (*winner*: Germany). **Preliminaries 2**: Russia 15, Georgia 9; Poland 23, Georgia 6; Russia 41, Poland 5 (*winner*: Russia). **Round-robin**: Romania 60, Germany 3; Russia 67, Germany 5; Romania 30, Russia 0 (*winner*: Romania).
EUROPEAN PLAY-OFFS: Romania 9, Wales 16; Italy 24, Romania 6; Wales 29, Italy 19 (rankings: 1. Wales; 2. Italy; 3. Romania).

ASIAN ZONE
Pool A: Malaysia 23, Sri Lanka 18; Japan 56, Chinese Taipei 5; Sri Lanka 3, Japan 67; Chinese Taipei 23, Malaysia 15; Malaysia 9, Japan 97; Chinese Taipei 25, Sri Lanka 9 (*winner*: Japan). **Pool B**: Hong Kong 17, Korea 28; Singapore 5, Thailand 69; Thailand 0, Hong Kong 93; Korea 90, Singapore 3; Singapore 13, Hong Kong 164; Korea 65, Thailand 13 (*winner*: Korea). **Play-off**: Hong Kong 80, Chinese Taipei 26. **Final**: Japan 26, Korea 11 (*winner*: Japan)

PACIFIC ZONE
Fiji 11, Tonga 24; Tonga 10, Fiji 15 (*winner*: Tonga).

AMERICAS ZONE
North: Bermuda 3, USA 60 (*winner*: USA). **South**: Chile 24, Paraguay 25; Paraguay 3, Uruguay 67; Uruguay 14, Chile 6; Argentina 70, Chile 7; Argentina 51, Paraguay 3; Uruguay 10, Argentina 19 (*winner*: Argentina). **Play-off**: USA 22, Argentina 28; Argentina 16, USA 11 (*winner*: Argentina).

AFRICAN ZONE SOUTH
Round-robin: Kenya 7, Zimbabwe 42; Namibia 64, Arabian Gulf 20; Kenya 9, Namibia 60; Zimbabwe 50, Arabian Gulf 21. **Play-off**: Kenya 24, Arabian Gulf 23. **Final**: Namibia 41, Zimbabwe 16 (*winners*: Namibia; *runners-up*: Zimbabwe).

AFRICAN ZONE NORTH
Round-robin: Tunisia 16, Ivory Coast 19; Tunisia 5, Morocco 6; Morocco 3, Ivory Coast 15 (*winners*: Ivory Coast; *runners-up*: Morocco).
AFRICAN PLAY-OFFS: Morocco 17, Ivory Coast 9; Namibia 25, Zimbabwe 20; Zimbabwe 21, Morocco 9; Ivory Coast 13, Namibia 12; Zimbabwe 10, Ivory Coast 17; Morocco 16, Namibia 16 (*winner*: Ivory Coast).

Hosts with a Point to Prove

SOUTH AFRICA

During the last World Cup, one of the enduring sights was a band of South African fans wandering around every stadium parading a banner with a Springbok on it and the words, "the real World Champions". It was an outlandish claim, but for the rest of the world there remained a nagging worry that it might just be true.

South Africa were banned from international competition at the time for apartheid in sport, of which rugby was possibly the most hard-line example. Yet with the start of the process of racial reconciliation shortly after the last World Cup, South Africa had an opportunity to show what they could do when they hosted touring parties from the two countries they most wanted to meet: world champions Australia and New Zealand, the benchmark by which South Africa judges itself.

A lot had changed since South Africa had been banished over a decade earlier. The game against New Zealand at Ellis Park was an eye opener, and although the Springboks rallied strongly in the last ten minutes to give an artificially close scoreline, the All Blacks were convincing victors. That late flurry convinced many South Africans that the match against the Australians would be different.

HARSH REALITY
All South Africa was looking forward to playing against Australia – the chance to beat the world champions and to prove the Springboks were worthy of that accolade. Yet it was a desire – verging on expectation – that took no account of quite how irked the Wallabies were to have their status questioned. In 80 riveting minutes at Loftus Versveld the South African dream was shattered. Australia took the Springboks apart.

Yet, ultimately, Australia did South Africa a favour. That defeat brought with it a sense of realism and meant that

subsequent defeats by France and England were not seen as the be-all and end-all by a rugby-mad public that now had its sights set on the 1995 World Cup.

Before isolation, they had a proud record – especially against the All Blacks – which placed them among the game's aristocracy. And with the resources South Africa have at their disposal, the hardest part of reintegration was in their coming to terms with the many law changes and differences in interpretation that had come about during isolation. Numerous penalties conceded, for lifting in the line-out and interfering

" It is virtually impossible to break down the Springbok defence. They are so well organised that even if you gain an advantage up front, the gaps do not appear in midfield. "

PHIL BENNETT,
FORMER WELSH FLY-HALF

with the ball on the floor at rucks, were two areas of concern, but the South Africans finally came to terms with these.

With international re-entry came a punishing schedule which paid dividends. As well as playing for the national side, the Super Ten competition meant that provincial players from the main Unions – Natal, Transvaal, Northern Transvaal, Western Province, Orange Free State and Eastern Province – were exposed to top level competition.

STRENGTH IN DEPTH

As a result, South Africa now have upwards of 60 players they can call on with Test or international experience. This strength in depth was evident on their late 1994 tour to Britain, as well as when they entertained England five months earlier. As both hosts and tourists, they completely outclassed their opponents.

The pre-isolation strength of the Springboks had always been in the forwards, but now it is their backs who have caught the eye. Big, strong, straight-running and hard-tackling, they have been difficult to contain for most of the sides that have met them over the past two years. On the hard grounds in South Africa, men like young scrum-half Joost van der Westhuizen, blockbusting centre Pieter Muller and magical fullback Andre Joubert – three players who did so much to put 78 points past Welsh champions Swansea on the tour of Wales – will be almost unstoppable.

The key to halting the Springboks is up front, and it is here that they have been working hardest. Indeed, it is only with the recent discovery of front jumper Mark Andrews that the South Africans have had a really effective line-out. But throw in a strong front row and an outstanding back row, in which number 8 Rudi Straueli and gritty openside Ruben Kruger are recent finds, and you have a pack able to compete on equal terms with any other in the world.

WORLD CUP RESULTS: *South Africa will be competing in the World Cup finals for the first time in 1995.*

The Springboks are the elite of the game in rugby-mad South Africa.

World Champions Looking to Pouch another Trophy

AUSTRALIA

Every country has its low point and for world champions Australia it was when they lost at home to Tonga in 1971. Losing many of its best players to big money offers from Rugby League, the Australians were struggling. So they looked to the best in the world – employing men like the great Welsh coach Carwyn James – and turned their game around.

Since then, Australia have gone from strength to strength and are now arguably the best rugby nation in the world. They still lose a steady flow of players to the professional code, which reigns supreme in Australia, but the doormat status they once endured is now a dim and distant memory.

Much of the credit for that transformation must go to two coaches, Alan Jones and Bob Dwyer. Jones coached the famous Grand Slam tour to Britain in 1984, when Australia ran riot through Britain. But Australia's promise was not fulfilled at the inaugural World Cup in 1987. Defeats against France in the tumultuous semi-final, and in the third-place play-off with Wales, signalled the end of Jones's reign.

Jones took the League dollar and was lost to the game. Bob Dwyer replaced him as the Australians' coach, but the

year, but the Lions were different. They came quite prepared to intimidate the Wallabies' pack and to disrupt halfbacks Nick Farr-Jones and Michael Lynagh to the point where they could contribute little to the game. It worked and it led to a reappraisal of the direction the Australians were taking.

BACK TO THE DRAWING BOARD

Rather than just produce a huge pack, captain Farr-Jones – the man on the receiving end of those uncompromising Lions tactics – demanded that Dwyer pick a side which could compete at that physical side. It was a task the coach set about immediately. Retaining Farr-Jones, fly-half Lynagh and wing David Campese as the core of the backs, Dwyer gave

> ❝ *Everything Australia have achieved has been based on their defence. They are the most difficult side in the world to break down.* ❞
>
> **MARK ELLA,**
> FORMER AUSTRALIA FLY-HALF

push to be the best in the world received another setback in the summer of 1989, when the British Lions came to Australia and left with a series victory under their belts. That series defeat proved to be a watershed in Australian rugby history.

Australia are used to bruising encounters, contesting the Bledisloe Cup with New Zealand every

Wallaby prop Tony Daly, who scored the winning try in the 1991 World Cup final.

WORLD CUP RESULTS

1987

England ....19 – 6
USA ....47 – 12
Japan ....42 – 23
Ireland (Quarter-final) ....33 – 15
France (Semi-final) ....24 – 30
Wales (Play-off) ....21 – 22

1991

Argentina ....32 – 19
Western Samoa.................9 – 3
Wales ....38 – 3
Ireland (Quarter-final) ....19 – 18
New Zealand (Semi-final) ......16 – 6
England (Play-off) ....12 – 6

youth its head and went about trying to find a young squad to compete at the next World Cup. Some luck was involved – Willie Ofahengaue was a New Zealand Colt tourist Australia who was refused entry back into his adopted country – but Dwyer also owed much to the Australian Institute of Sport (AIS) which identified young players at an early stage. It was here that Dwyer found outstanding young centres Tim Horan and Jason Little, as well as lock John Eales, the outstanding line-out jumper in world rugby. Dwyer also looked for men with the physical attributes, plucking players like hooker Phil Kearns – then a club third-team player – out of obscurity.

SUCCESS BREEDS SUCCESS

It was a plan that worked like a dream and is self-perpetu-ating. There is hardly a weak link in the side, despite the retirement of Farr-Jones and a horrific knee injury to Tim Horan, widely regarded as one of the best centres in the world. Up front, the front row of McKenzie, Kearns and Daly bows to no man, while the three line-out jumpers – veteran Rod McCall, the inspirational Eales and number 8 Tim Gavin – provide a wealth of quality ball. In the loose, Willie Ofahengaue is simply enormous, and openside David Wilson is a gritty fighter.

The backs are superbly marshalled by captain Lynagh, and have Campese to call upon for inspiration in times of need – such as in the 1991 World Cup semi-final against New Zealand. Their superb drift defence means they con-cede few points, while their flat alignment in attack, coupled with great speed and some prodigious young talents, means that they can destroy loose defences

Defending their title will not be easy, especially as they have been drawn to meet hosts South Africa in the opening game of the tournament, while the rest of the "group of death" – Canada and Romania – will provide stern tests.

Australia's line-out wonderkid John Eales.

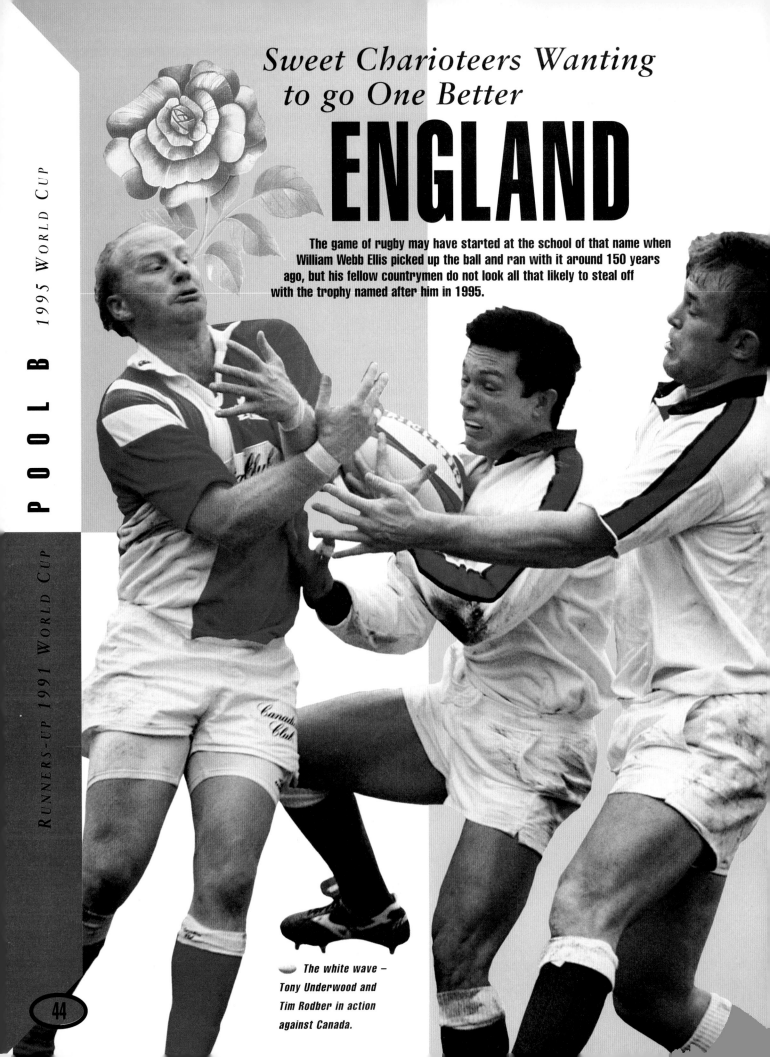

Sweet Charioteers Wanting to go One Better

ENGLAND

The game of rugby may have started at the school of that name when William Webb Ellis picked up the ball and ran with it around 150 years ago, but his fellow countrymen do not look all that likely to steal off with the trophy named after him in 1995.

The white wave –
Tony Underwood and
Tim Rodber in action
against Canada.

England don't travel particularly well and have not been successful on recent trips to play the best that the rugby world has to offer. In South Africa, in the middle of 1994, with the exception of 20 glorious minutes in the First Test which they won, they played well below their best. And in Australia, shortly before the 1991 World Cup, they lost by a record 40–15 to Australia.

Their game is suited to the wet and windy conditions that prevail in the Northern Hemisphere. They have a huge pack that revels in the tight loose and can grapple with the best of them. Show England a situation where they can grind down an opposing pack and there are very few sides in the world who can live with them.

However, when a more expansive game is called for, they are simply not used to playing that sort of football. It's not that they don't have the players – they do. But when England tried changing to a more free-flowing game in the last World Cup final, they could not do it.

> *England have a pool of players every other nation is extremely envious of. Yet they will only prosper if the harsh lessons learnt on the tour to South Africa have been taken on board.*
>
> **ROGER UTTLEY,**
> FORMER ENGLAND PLAYER AND COACH

THE WRONG GAME PLAN
And on the rock-hard grounds of South Africa, where England will face opponents used to playing 15-man rugby, and used to playing in broken play situations, they may again struggle. New England manager Jack Rowell saw on 1994's tour to South Africa how ill-equipped England's naturally conservative players are at handling the running style, and he has tried to instill a more expansive game plan. Six months is not long for England's players to absorb what for others is second nature.

LINE-OUT LUXURY
Even so, if Rowell can teach England to think on their feet they will be very difficult to beat. At the line-out they have many tall trees to choose from: Nigel Redman or Martin Johnson at the front; Simon Shaw or Martin Bayfield at the middle; and Ben Clarke or Tim Rodber at the back. Along with a solid scrummage, they should win at least half of set-piece ball, and a team that does that is always in with a fighting chance.

By far the most interesting area of England's side, though, is the back row. The problem – if Jack Rowell could

🏉 *Old Dependable – veteran England hooker Brian Moore passes the ball to new scrum-half Kyran Bracken.*

call it that – is that he has too many outstanding number 8s. Ben Clarke, Dean Richards, Tim Rodber and Steve Ojomoh are all pushing for a place and all are worthy of a place in almost any international side. Yet the problem is one of balance – three huge men in a back row is just one too many when the game will be played fast and hard on bone dry pitches, so Richards may lose out.

BACKS TO THE FORE
In the backs, England have, in Jeremy Guscott and Rory Underwood, two of the most scintillating attackers in modern rugby. Fly-half Rob Andrew is superb at keeping a winning pack going forward, while the defence of scrum-half Dewi Morris and captain Will Carling at centre means that they have an enormously miserly defence.

Will Carling has openly admitted that he believes England are not capable of beating either New Zealand, Australia or South Africa over a three-Test series, but that he believes they can raise their game to beat any of the Southern Hemisphere giants in a one-off game. Given that the World Cup is in effect a series of one-offs, England are certainly a team to watch and are definitely one of the sides every other major nation fears playing.

WORLD CUP RESULTS

1987

Australia		6 – 19
Japan		60 – 7
USA		34 – 6
Wales *(Quarter-final)*		3 – 16

1991

New Zealand		12 – 18
Italy		36 – 6
USA		37 – 9
France *(Quarter-final)*		19 – 10
Scotland *(Semi-final)*		9 – 6
Australia *(Final)*		6 – 12

All Blacks from the Land of the Silver Fern

NEW ZEALAND

NEW ZEALAND
ALL BLACKS

There is a benchmark by which every international side judges itself – the All Blacks. They are the most consistent side in the world. With a population for whom the game is almost a religion, every top Kiwi player is technically perfect, and that is reflected in the national side. With such a deep pool of talent, there has never been a bad All Black side, and to beat the New Zealanders is a supreme feat.

"I believe we have the players, the infrastructure and the expertise to win the next World Cup."

JOHN HART,
FORMER NEW ZEALAND COACH

The Haka, an intimidating Maori challenge, is performed before All Black matches.

The name "All Blacks" originates from an early tour to Britain, when a newspaper reported that the New Zealanders were so versatile they "played like all backs" and the nickname stuck. Even then, New Zealand was infected with rugby fever and produced teams like 1924's "Invincibles", whose tour of Britain ended up as an exercise in damage limitation for the home sides.

The Invincibles were also unique in that they made up their own Haka, the Maori war dance that the All Blacks now perform before each game as a challenge to their opponents. Since then, every

🏉 *All Black charge – Centre Frank Bunce leads the way in the series win over the British Lions in the summer of 1993.*

New Zealand side has used the original version of the Haka, which starts with the words "kamate, kamate" which, roughly translated, means "it is death, it is death."

· The Haka is a symbol of just how important the Maoris are to New Zealand rugby, and such is their strength that the Maori XV almost defeated the British Lions in 1993.

TACTICAL INNOVATORS

New Zealand rugby has a hard edge to it that comes from its rural background. Many former All Blacks were from farming stock, and their style of play reflects that – hard, no frills, driving play. But because the game is so important to

the Kiwis, they are also great thinkers and were the first to perfect the rucking game, and to adopt the rolling maul.

But whatever style of play the All Blacks adopt, they always play superbly well. Efficiency is their hallmark, and sentimentality an anathema. Rugby is New Zealand's way of keeping in touch with the rest of the world, so winning is everything. That is why it meant so much to the Kiwis to win the first World Cup in 1987. Not that it was in doubt. The mid-1980s team was as good as any Test side has ever been, and with names like Shelford, Mexted, Kirwan, Fox and Gallagher in the equation, the competition was an unequal contest from beginning to end, David Kirk duly lifting the Trophy after beating France in the inaugural final.

UNSUCCESSFUL DEFENCE

Four years later, though, it was a different story. In a most un-Kiwi like way, several players past their prime were allowed to linger. There was still enough gas in the engine to see off England, but not to do the same to Australia and David Campese in Dublin in a match which the Wallabies had effectively won by half-time.

While the current New Zealand side is not in the same class as that of 1987, it will nevertheless be one of the sides to beat. It has already seen off the Springboks and the British Lions in the 1993 and 1994. However, the All Blacks did lose the Bledisloe Cup (the annual series with Australia), as well as to England and France.

The defection of John Timu to League was also a major blow, as was the failure to establish a settled halfback partnership following Grant Fox's retirement and the fact that only young wing Jeff Wilson has much Test experience. The All Blacks nevertheless retain one of the most exciting back divisions in the tournament, with centre Frank Bunce the standout, while any pack led by Sean Fitzpatrick will always pull its weight.

WORLD CUP RESULTS

🏉 1987 🏉

Italy	70 – 6
Fiji	74 – 13
Argentina	46 – 15
Scotland *(Quarter-final)*	30 – 3
Wales *(Semi-final)*	49 – 6
France *(Final)*	29 – 9

🏉 1991 🏉

England	18 – 12
USA	46 – 6
Italy	31 – 21
Canada *(Quarter-final)*	29 – 13
Australia *(Semi-final)*	6 – 16
Scotland *(Play-off)*	13 – 6

Prickly Customers Hoping to Bloom

SCOTLAND

Kenny Logan goes for broke.

Semi-finalists at the last World Cup, Scotland are in trouble. Slaughtered at home by New Zealand and thumped by South Africa, the unfortunate Scots even lost both Tests on their developmental summer tour to Argentina. Throw in a wooden spoon in 1993–94's Five Nations Championship and the added negative of playing the World Cup 5,000 miles from Murrayfield, and you have an idea of the sort of progress Scotland will need to make if they are to avoid a Welsh-style debacle in South Africa.

Yet Scotland are nothing if not fighters, a fact illustrated by the last tournament when they met England at Murrayfield in the semi-final. Despite having a woefully underpowered scrum – and consequently being under pressure from beginning to end – Scotland were disruptive in defence, tenacious in attack and almost stole the match. But for Gavin Hastings's penalty miss from straight in front of the posts, it could well have been Scotland on their way to Twickenham to meet the Australians.

They match typified the way the Scots like – or at least need – to play the game: fast rucking followed by quick release and a hoof for the forwards to chase. Not too pretty, but it has worked often enough in the past and has the virtue of not needing a huge pack to be effective (this is particularly useful as Scotland rarely if ever have huge packs – and now is no different).

It was certainly a tactic that worked for the Scots against the Springboks in the provincial games. "It just goes to show what can be achieved by good technique," said South African scrum-half Kevin Putt. "The Scots might be small but they ruck better than any team I have ever seen."

NEW TACTICS NEEDED

Reality, however, should intrude at this point. It's all very well rucking like demons on a paddy field in the Borders on a wet winter afternoon, but with the probability of the sun blazing down on a dustbowl at the tip of the dark continent things will soon look a little less rosy.

After the last World Cup, they lost influential figures such as John Jeffrey, Derek White, David Sole, Finlay Calder, Sean Lineen and Iwan Tukalo. Players of that calibre have yet to be replaced, while scrum-half Gary Armstrong has a broken leg which will keep him out of South Africa and the Hastings brothers, fullback Gavin and centre Scott, are not the force they once were.

WORLD CUP RESULTS

1987

France	20 – 20
Zimbabwe	60 – 21
Romania	55 – 28
New Zealand *(Quarter-final)*	3 – 30

1991

Japan	47 – 9
Zimbabwe	51 – 12
Ireland	24 – 15
Western Samoa *(Quarter-final)*	28 – 6
England *(Semi-final)*	6 – 9
New Zealand *(Play-off)*	6 – 13

SCRUMMAGING BLUES

The whole scenario suggests worrying times ahead for the captain Gavin Hastings and coach Morgan. However, it is not a situation without hope. The main springboard if they are to do well must be the back row. This is the one area where they have talent in abundance. The optimum back row would probably be the ever-impressive Rob Wainwright at blindside – providing he can keep injury free – with beanpole Doddie Weir at number 8 and Iain Morrison at openside. It may be a light back row, but it is also a very mobile one, which will be well suited to harder grounds and to moving the ball away from contact situations as soon as they develop.

The weak link will be the front five and their inability to win first-phase possession. The presence of Weir will be a valuable asset at the line-out, as will Andy Reed if he is on song; yet the best Scotland can really hope for here is parity – and even then they will be doing very well. The scrummage may well be a problem if Alan Sharp's otherwise fine skills are overshadowed by his penchant for collapsing – an offence sure to be penalised heavily by referees at the World Cup. In November 1994's mauling from South Africa, the scrum found itself being pushed back metres at a time.

The backs are likely to suffer from a shortage of ball from first and second-phase, while whoever plays fly-half – be it Gregor Townsend or Craig Chalmers – will find out that what is termed an up-and-under at home is called kicking away possession elsewhere. With the Scots' general lack of pace likely to prove a real problem in defence, wings Kenny Logan and Craig Joiner are probably the only Scottish backs who will enjoy their first taste of playing rugby on the concrete that passes for pitches in South Africa.

> **"Scotland have a problem. The cream of one generation has called it a day, while that of the next generation has yet to rise to the surface."**
>
> **RICHARD PEMBROKE,**
> *RUGBY NEWS MAGAZINE*

Second row Damian Cronin turns and sets against South Africa.

Unpredictables from North America

Rugby CANADA

Canada will be remembered as one of the revelations of the 1991 World Cup largely thanks to a gutsy display in Lille, when they pushed the All Blacks near to breaking point in the second half of a rain-sodden quarter-final. Although they were already beaten, the brave way the Canucks took the fight to the defending World Champions in a memorable second-half display, beating them at their own game up front, seemed to prove that a new force had finally emerged at the top-level as a nation at last capable of challenging the "Big Eight".

Colin McKenzie makes headway against England.

If anything, the performance against New Zealand was no more than confirmation that Canada's pre-tournament and pool form was not a flash in the pan. And it was a formidably impressive road to the finals for one of world rugby's most ambitious nations. Not only had they surprisingly topped the Americas qualifying group ahead of Argentina – by beating the almost impregnable Pumas at home in a clash of unremitting intensity in Buenos Aires – but Canada had also beaten a Scotland Development side.

It was against this background of consistent achievement against quality international opposition that Canada entered the World Cup. And, as with Western Samoa, the only people to be surprised by their ability to compete in this elevated company was the elevated company itself. Their last World Cup campaign showed how important pitting themselves against the best had been, and it was this experience that allowed the Canadians to edge tight encounters against Romania and Fiji.

INTERNATIONAL COMING OF AGE

The first hint that they could really challenge the best came in Agen when they pushed France all the way before eventually succumbing 19-13. As Canadian team manager Mike Luke said after the tournament: "The symbol of our coming

On hallowed ground – while the Canadians did not win on their first visit to Twickenham, they are World Cup dark horses.

"The greatest pleasure of all is that none of what we have achieved has been the product of luck. We have a side capable of beating the best, and that is a genuine reflection of the strength in depth in Canadian rugby."

MIKE LUKE,
CANADA'S MANAGER AT THE 1991 WORLD CUP

of age in the tournament was the fight between French prop Pascal Ondarts and our scrum-half Chris Tynan. When I saw Tynan taking punches and then answering back in kind, I realised that our attempt to establish ourselves as a top playing nation had succeeded."

Since then, Canada have claimed a couple of notable scalps – they beat Wales at the National Stadium in 1993 and France in Canada in 1994 – but have yet to convince anyone that they can really make the transition to a top flight Test nation.

LEARNING FROM MISTAKES

The doubters got a further boost when the Canadians arrived to play England in December 1994, and got beaten, 60–19, on their first visit to Twickenham. It may have been devastating to lose a match they had high hopes of winning by such an emphatic margin, yet the Canadians have got where they are precisely because they have the capacity to learn from their mistakes. Rob Andrew's boot and a couple of interceptions apart, the main reason for the size of the

loss was the conscious effort to play a more expansive game. According to coach Ian Birtwell: "This meant that in the course of trying to push back quicker ball, we were too loose and lost the ball several times in contact when we would not normally have expected to."

The bulk of the Canadian national side come from the Vancouver Island area of British Columbia, where the style is very forward-orientated. Former Wallaby lock Peter FitzSimons gave a pretty good indication of the way the game is played there when he recalled a past tour there: "The local boys are particularly notable for the ferocity of their forward rushes."

Canada's success has been built on a formidable pack in which the propping partnership of Dan Jackart and Eddie Evans has been outstanding. Other world-class Canadian forwards include gigantic second row Norm Hadley, number 8 Al Charron and 36-year-old open-side flanker Gord MacKinnon. Yet Canada also have the raw materials to succeed in their attempts to play a more expansive game. Halfbacks John Graf and Gareth Rees both possess talent and experience, while fullback Scott Stewart has ruined more than one career with some of the most aggressive offensive tackling in world rugby. And wing David Lougheed – who scored two tries at Twickenham – is one of the most accomplished wide men in the modern game.

WORLD CUP RESULTS

1987	
Tonga	37 – 4
Ireland	19 – 46
Wales	9 – 40

1991	
Fiji	13 – 3
Romania	19 – 11
France	13 – 19
New Zealand *(Quarter-final)*	13 – 29

Peerless stylists of the Northern Hemisphere

FRANCE

When rugby people think of France, a whole range of emotions come to the mind. As a rugby-playing nation, France are best characterised as the good, the bad, and the downright ugly. The good is their fantastic flair and their love for the running and handling parts of the game.

When France hit a purple patch, they are capable of playing rugby like no other side on earth. It is marvellous to watch and can result in some spectacular tries. One memorable example of this was in the 1991 Five Nations Grand Slam decider against England at Twickenham, when fullback Serge Blanco broke from behind his own line, switched the ball left and started off a move that ended with wing Philippe St Andre touching down to rapturous applause for a brilliant try. Indeed, St Andre was also involved in another of the all-time great tries in New Zealand in 1994 when, with France having won the First Test and the All Blacks leading narrowly in the Second, the French launched a counter-attack from their own line. It was one of the most stunning movements ever constructed, with the ball passing between six pairs of hands until Jean-Luc Sadourny dived over to claim the first series win in New Zealand by a Northern hemisphere side. It was, said St Andre, "a try from the end of the earth."

That series win turned France from wannabees into real contenders for the World Cup. They had already won series in South Africa and in Australia, so that miraculous series win was proof positive that France could beat any of the Southern Hemisphere giants on the road. They are the only Northern Hemisphere side to have done so, and have a game which is perfectly suited to South Africa.

DISCIPLINE IMPROVES

The New Zealand series also had another side effect – it conclusively buried the bad and ugly sides of the French psyche. Over the years, the indiscipline, a tendency to give away penalties and allowing frustration to boil over into violence has cost the French many internationals. It was a weakness in their game that was ruthlessly exploited by the other top sides. Yet in this series, France held their nerve and concentration in the most physical and bruising of encounters and did not leak points from penalties in the way they had on previous occasions. In fact, the French discipline showed itself in all areas. They have developed a single-mindedness and ability to play it tight if necessary which bodes well for South Africa.

> **"*France have the talent and technique to challenge any side. They are confident and equipped to cope with all the demands of a World Cup.*"**
>
> **MIKE GIBSON,**
> FORMER IRELAND CENTRE

France have invariably produced monster packs, but they have had few in recent times as well balanced as this one. They have a strong-scrummaging front row in which hooker Jean-Michel Gonzales is a pillar of strength in the tight, while bald loosehead prop Laurent Benezech is outstanding in the loose. A phenomenally strong tight five is completed by second rows Olivier Merle, a mean 20 stone (127kg) former lumberjack who took up rugby for a bet after he lost a game of dice, and Olivier Roumat, the precocious Dax lock who has become one of the most accomplished number four line-out jumpers in the game.

High rise Roumat – the French line-out jumper soars.

ALL-AROUND POWER

They are complemented by a back row which is both big and fast. Abdel Benazzi, a 6ft 6in (2m) Moroccan, is a strong-mauling forward and a force to reckon with at the back of the line-out, while Philippe Benetton also adds bulk and speed. Lanky openside flanker Laurent Cabannes also has the world's highest jump at the tail of the line-out.

It is a tremendously well-balanced pack which links well with an exciting back line. Scrum-half Guy Accoceberry is workmanlike, but his skills are well matched with the more eccentric talents of inventive fly-half Christophe Deylaud. At centre, France boast a formidably physical part-nership in 100-cap veteran Philippe Sella and the burly Thierry Lacroix, while wing and captain Philippe St Andre and fullback Jean-Luc Sadourny provide the flair.

It is, above all else, a tried and tested side with a proven track record and the right style to suceed in South Africa. They had a tendency to lose games they should win – such as at home to Argentina and away to Canada – but they are the most likely of the Northern Hemisphere sides to push for top spot at the World Cup.

WORLD CUP RESULTS

1 9 8 7

Scotland	20 – 20
Romania	55 – 12
Zimbabwe	70 – 12
Fiji *(Quarter-final)*	31 – 16
Australia *(Semi-final)*	30 – 24
New Zealand *(Final)*	9 – 29

1 9 9 1

Romania	30 – 3
Fiji	33 – 9
Canada	19 – 13
England *(Quarter-final)*	10 – 19

Don't mess with us – France's front row is one the many strong points of the current team.

Popular Competitors from the Emerald Isle

IRELAND

The Irish are uniquely liked in world rugby. Gracious tourists and wonderful hosts, there is nothing most sides like more than to play the Irish or – even better – visit the Emerald Isle itself. Unfortunately, much of the reason for that of late has been the national side's weakness.

With the smallest playing numbers of any of the major countries, Ireland have always struggled to put out the sort of side to compete with England, France, New Zealand, South Africa or any of the other major playing nations. And while the indomitable Irish spirit means that their numerical handicaps haven't always counted against them, it is nevertheless true that they can pull out the stops on the big occasion.

Ireland were involved in the most exciting game of the last World Cup. Played at Dublin's Lansdowne Road, the quarter-final against Australia had the crowd enraptured throughout. It was an awesome game in which Ireland's traditional "up-and-at-'em" philosophy got them far further than anyone had hoped or expected. Indeed, with just over five minutes left, Ireland flanker Gordon Hamilton broke free and tore 60 metres down the left touchline for a try which everyone in the ground thought had put Ireland into the semi-final. But it was not to be: Australia stole the game on the final whistle through a Michael Lynagh try.

NEW COMPETITIVENESS

Yet all is not as it once was in Irish rugby. The advent of the All Ireland League has meant a hardening of attitudes, and almost every player in the country is (and whisper this quietly now) training hard all year round. Gone are the Guinness diets, in are pasta, fresh fruit and fish. Organisationally, Ireland are still lagging far behind the world's leaders, yet they have now developed a core of committed players and the current side has 10 of top-class international quality – about three or four more than at any stage since the last World Cup.

Yet some things never change in Irish rugby, and the importance of the front row is one of them. This was the phase of the game around which the Ireland teams of old based their entire game plan, and while the scrum no longer has quite the same tactical importance, it is now Ireland's strongest area.

WORLD'S BEST FRONT THREE

When the South Africans – who pride themselves on their scrummaging – met the Barbarians in Dublin in December 1994, the invitation side fielded the full Irish front row. The results were breathtaking: the Springboks were shoved metres backwards at least four times and they were under pressure throughout. The tighthead prop Peter Clohessy, hooker Keith Wood and loosehead prop Nick Popplewell form as good a front row as is to be found in world rugby. Not only are they formidable at the set-piece, but they are always in support in the loose, where Wood and Popplewell in particular are outstanding.

Behind that front row, Ireland have also managed to build some strength in depth. Second row Neil Francis is a prodigiously talented line-out jumper, while either Paddy Johns or Gabriel Fulcher can make a decent fist of jumping at the front.

Ireland's awesome front row of (left to right) Peter Clohessy, Keith Wood and Nick Popplewell.

> **"** *A game which is structured in its entirety does not suit Irish instincts. It slows the mind and dulls the spirit. Ireland need unpredictability and an element of disorder – purposeful chaos.* **"**

MIKE GIBSON,
LEGENDARY IRELAND CENTRE

AUSTRALIAN TOUR HEROES

The back row has been strengthened by the discovery of flanker David Corkery, a big man who will prosper in South Africa. Corkery was just one of three discoveries that have given cause for optimism. The other two were Wood and utility back Jonathan Bell.

Bell is a player of immense talent, who coach Jerry Murphy likened to Tim Horan after the Australian adventure. He will probably play on the wing, but could grace the back line anywhere. The real star of the show is frantic blond wing Simon Geoghegan, possibly the best wide man in the world.

With veteran centre Brendan Mullin coming out of retirement to partner another veteran, former captain Phil Danaher, Ireland are now very close to having a well-rounded side able to compete in all departments. The biggest problem comes at halfback, where scrum-half and captain Michael Bradley's erratic passing puts a lot of pressure on fly-half and place-kicker Eric Elwood.

Irish prop Nick Popplewell drives into the US Eagles' defence in Ireland's late 1994 win at Lansdowne Road.

WORLD CUP RESULTS

1987

Wales	6 – 13
Canada	46 – 19
Tonga	32 – 9
Australia *(Quarter-final)*	15 – 33

1991

Zimbabwe	55 – 11
Japan	32 – 16
Scotland	15 – 24
Australia *(Quarter-final)*	18 – 19

Brave Fighters from the Pacific Islands

WESTERN SAMOA

The history of Western Samoan rugby at international level is a very recent one. Although Western Samoa toured Wales in the early 1980s and there has been a side in the Pacific Championship every year, as well as one at the Hong Kong Sevens, the serious marshalling of resources only began in the run-up to the 1991 World Cup. It was then that former All Black wing Bryan Williams, one of a long line of Samoans to play for New Zealand, was drafted in, along with fellow exile Peter Schuster, to mastermind the Samoan World Cup campaign.

Samoan rugby enjoys a symbiotic relationship with New Zealand and, to a lesser extent, Australia, with most players who really want to achieve something in the game moving to Auckland or Sydney in the hope of gaining an All Black or Wallaby cap. So it was to New Zealand that Williams and Schuster turned. They knew that they could find players there who were desperate to make the breakthrough into international rugby.

The building block of the side was an ageing Auckland prop Peter "Fats" Fatialofa, and he was joined by flanker Apollo Perelini, who had played for the New Zealand Colts, while number 8 Pat Lam, centre Frank Bunce, wing Timo "The Tank" Tagaloa and fly-half Steven Bachop had all either played for an All Black XV or for the national sevens side.

THE SHAPE OF THINGS TO COME
Williams and Schuster also combed the Antipodes looking for players who could help them overcome one of the main problems in putting together a truly competitive Samoan

Test side – the Polynesian physique. While the Fijians may have lots of tall, rangy players, the Samoans tend to be squatter and heavier. They are a huge-boned race, whose physique is absolutely perfect for rampaging three-quarters and bone-crushing flankers, but is much less useful for producing talented and agile line-out jumpers.

The search for Samoan grandparents, however, turned up qualifications for dour Aucklander Matt Keenan and a young tyro called Mark Birtwhistle. Put together

WORLD CUP RESULTS

1991

Wales	16 – 13
Australia	3 – 9
Argentina	35 – 12
Scotland *(Quarter-final)*	6 – 28

> **"***The victory over Wales in the last World Cup gave us our place in the sun – but I have been amazed at how well we have been able to stay there.***"**
>
> **BRYAN WILLIAMS,**
> WESTERN SAMOA'S COACH

Junior Tonuu gets the ball away against Canada as Western Samoa win the Hong Kong Sevens title in 1993.

Sam Kaleta drives into the Welsh defence during Samoa's victory over the tourists in the middle of 1994.

with a particularly effective back row pool that included Lam, Perelini, Junior Paramore and Sila Vaifale, the Samoans had a pack to reckon with. And with backs of the calibre of Bachop, Bunce and Tagaloa, Samoa were set.

WORLD CUP HEROES

What happened at the last World Cup is now well-known. Western Samoa beat Wales and Argentina and pushed Australia to the limit in the mud at Pontypool Park before going out in the quarter-final to Scotland at Murrayfield. Their offensive tackling was the talk of the tournament, and their "Manu Samoa" challenge – their equivalent to New Zealand's Haka – one of its enduring memories.

To understand what it meant to Samoa as a whole, you have only to read the words of captain Fatialofa on the team's return home. "Rugby is a very important sport in Samoa – it is our national sport and it is in the blood of our children who start playing on the beach with coconuts before they touch a ball at all," he said.

"To understand what all this meant for Samoa, you should have been in Apia on the Saturday when we arrived back. I had tears in my eyes when I saw the 20 miles of road between the airport and Apia lined with thousands of cheering Samoans. The celebrations were awesome and the reception in the national stadium was attended by 50,000 people, one third of the country's population. The boys were staggered and so was I."

CONTINUING THE PROGRESS

But as Bryan Williams was the first to recognise, getting there is one thing – staying there is quite another. Since the last World Cup, Samoa have lost many of their stars. Perelini has gone off to play League, while Bunce and Bachop have established themselves as All Blacks.

Yet the inroads that were made in 1991 have, on the whole, been maintained. Lam still plays for Samoa and in fly-half Darren Kellet they have uncovered a gem of a number 10 with a cultured boot. Competition in the Super 10 has shown them what they need to do if they are to remain competitive without the benefit of surprise, and they have emerged as the strongest Pacific Island side. They comprehensively beat tourists Scotland and Wales, and pushed New Zealand all the way in Auckland. In fact, apart from a freak 75-point loss to Australia, Samoa have proved they are a force to reckon with.

Travelling More in Hope than Expectation

ARGENTINA

Argentina has a proud tradition of being the most difficult place in the rugby world to tour, and for producing the poorest tourists in world rugby. Tour Argentina and you will be lucky to escape unscathed, but play Argentine tourists and the chances are it will be a pretty comfortable 80 minutes.

The Pumas' inability to reproduce their home form on foreign fields is the prime reason for their disappointing World Cup record to date. If they didn't perform well in 1987, their 1991 form was even more worrying: three played and three lost, and without even the hint of a win, if the truth be told. Western Samoa, Wales and Australia all ended up reasonably comfortable winners over Argentina.

Yet an inability to play well away from home is not the only reason for the Pumas' barren spell over the past eight years. They could also point to the debilitating effects of the drift to Italy of many of their top players. The staunchly amateur Argentine Union was (and is) convinced that its players were being paid to go and play in Italy and promptly banned over 100 of them. They included such seasoned performers as prop Serafin Dengra, scrum-half Fabio Gomez and fly-half-cum-centre Diego Dominguez.

A BRIGHTER FUTURE

The recovery period has clearly been a long one, but there is a case for thinking that Argentina are becoming competitive at the top level once again. They retain their famous scrummaging power, and while their line-out remains substandard, they are producing more mobile back row players than ever before.

Behind the scrum, they have several classy players: most notably the midfield pairing of scrum-half Gonzalo

Quick getaway – Argentina scrum-half Rafael Bullrich in action against South Africa.

"The win in France showed at last that we can win away from home. That has given us great heart for the next World Cup."

MARTIN TERAN,
PUMAS WING

Camardon and fly-half Lisandru Arbizu, and wing Martin Teran. They have also – belatedly – begun to win away from home and recorded a shock win over France in 1992, the first ever by an Argentine side on French soil. They also have a youthful side, who are used to playing on the sort of hard surfaces they will find in South Africa.

WORLD CUP RESULTS

1987

Fiji	9 – 28
Italy	25 – 16
New Zealand	15 – 46

1991

Australia	19 – 32
Wales	7 – 16
Western Samoa	12 – 35

Mediterranean Contenders with Mercurial Talents

ITALY

Outside of the Five Nations, the next best country in Europe is Italy. Even though rugby is played throughout Northern Italy, the game has still to catch on as a massively popular game there. However, the influx of top-class foreign players in domestic rugby has markedly improved its standard. And in their coach, Australian Mark Ella, they have a man of immense vision.

Ella's task had been made easier because the squad he inherited from Bertrand Fourcarde after the last World Cup had tasted some success, having convincingly beaten the USA, and pushed New Zealand all the way in their 31–21 loss. Only against England, when they cynically tried to kill the game by infringing constantly, were they unimpressive.

The side has a solid scrummage, a good line-out and some players of genuine talent behind the forwards. Chief among those are wing Marcello Cuttitta, Argentine-born, super kicking fly-half Diego Dominguez, fullback Paolo Vaccari and utility back Ivan Francescato. Cuttitta has been injured but the experienced wing – who learnt his trade as a youngster living in Natal – is a proven try-scorer who can live in any company.

Roberto Favaro – secures possession in the World Cup qualifying win over Romania.

> **"There are a lot of very good players in Italy. They can push any side in the world."**
>
> DAVID CAMPESE,
> AUSTRALIAN WING WHO PLAYS HIS CLUB RUGBY IN ITALY

HOME-GROWN TALENT

Francescato is such a talented player that Ella has moved him to the wing, because such is his influence that he imposes his game on the national side rather than the other way around if he plays at scrum-half. Both he and Vaccari, a strong-running pocket battleship, are proven try-scorers.

Up front Italy are equally competitive. Their scrum is immovably anchored by Massimo Cuttitta, brother of Marcello, while Favaro and Checchinato provide a constant source of ball from the line-out. Australian born Julian Gardner provides the edge in loose play.

Italy beat the Romania well and thought they should have beaten Wales in Cardiff. They should also have beaten Australia in both Tests when they toured there in 1994, then their B side beat the full Canada side just before Christmas.

WORLD CUP RESULTS

1987

New Zealand		6 – 70
Argentina		16 – 25
Fiji		18 – 15

1991

USA		30 – 9
England		6 – 36
New Zealand		21 – 31

Surprise Qualifiers from the Gulf of Guinea
IVORY COAST

It remains the most spectacular upset in the history of the World Cup qualifiers. Namibia, the darling of the emerging nations of Southern Africa, had expected the African zone qualifying tournament to be a triumphant procession, with them emerging to make their World Cup debuts in South Africa. But it was not to be.

However, nobody told that to the Ivory Coast. In the heat of the qualifying tournament held in Casablanca it was the Ivory Coast, who came through as the surprise winners after they unexpectedly beat Zimbabwe before going on to scrape through by a single point against the much-fancied Namibians.

Just four years earlier at the Harare qualifying tournament, the Ivory Coast's game against the Moroccans had been abandoned because of on-field violence. And this time around, the Ivory Coast were again willing to intimidate and hustle in their bid to get to the World Cup finals. Despite losing to hosts Morocco in their opener, the game that really mattered was against Namibia.

FAVOURITES UPSET
In a desperate match, French-based Ivory Coast prop Touissant Djehi led the intimidation, and although the Namibians saved the match from degenerating into the sort of chaos seen four years earlier at Harare, they ceded the initiative – and the match – to their less experienced rivals.

Yet the Ivory Coast will have more to offer than aggression in South Africa. The game in the former French colony was exported from the South of France, but has now assumed a life of its own and club games there can now draw up to 15,000 spectators. Their game is heavily influenced by the French and many of their players play for French clubs, while coaches Claude Ezoua and Dominique Davanier come from France.

This goes a long way to explaining the strengths in the Ivory Coast's game – an impressive rolling maul, a good line-out, and exciting back play – but also accounts for an attitude that can verge on the cynical. One thing is certain, unless captain Athanse Dali improves his goal-kicking they will return without a win.

> **"We didn't see it, but they are actually quite a good side. And they are certainly very physical."**
>
> **GERHARD MANS,**
> NAMIBIAN CAPTAIN

The Ivory Coast front row on their way to World Cup qualification.

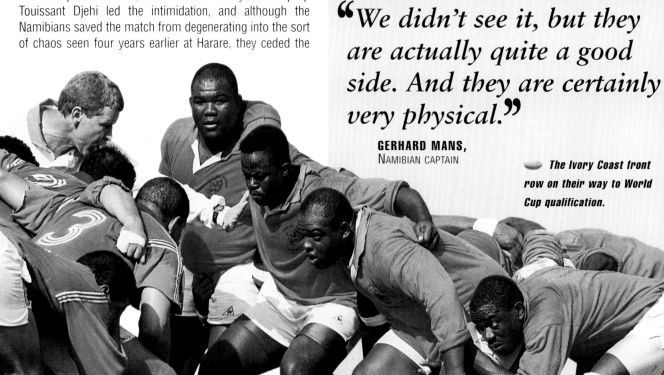

WORLD CUP RESULTS: *Ivory Coast will be competing in the World Cup finals for the first time in 1995.*

Asian Champions with a Mountain to Climb

JAPAN

It says much about the Japanese, and about the game of rugby itself, that it is the second most popular team sport in Japan after baseball even though Japan will always remain also-rans in world terms. For no matter whatever else can change in rugby, one fact remains constant – that a good big 'un will always beat a good little 'un. And the Japanese are not big.

"With reasonable possession, we can do a lot with the ball. But the line-out gives us real cause for concern – and I really cannot see that changing."

SHIGGY KONNO,
JAPANESE RUGBY SUPREMO

It has always been the dearest wish of Shiggy Konno, the godfather of Japanese rugby, that the rest of the world would stand still for 20 years so that the extra inches Japanese youngsters are piling on would stand them in better stead rather than simply maintaining the status quo.

For the moment, though, the Japanese are attempting to get around the problem of having a minute pack by shoring up their back five with a couple of Tongans and a Taiwanese player. Although they will never find themselves dominating up front, the Japanese rightly feel that if they can win even a third of ball, then they are in with a chance. This

His greatest moment – Japan's fullback Takahiro Hosokawa goes over for a try against Scotland in 1991.

was certainly the case at the last World Cup, when the input of the two Tongans in their back row – Sinali Latu and Ekeroma Tifaga – helped them overcome a much larger Zimbabwe side 52–8.

HIGH NUMBERS BEST

And Japan have had their successes, most notably against Scotland in 1989, while they regularly beat the hefty Europeans who turn out for Hong Kong to win the Asian Championships each year. That said, it is unlikely that they will do anything other than make up the numbers when they arrive in South Africa.

If they can win some ball, they undoubtedly have the potential to trouble any back line in the tournament. Certainly they were no walkovers when Ireland and Scotland met them in the last World Cup, and Ireland only won by 32–16. The two wings, diminutive flier Yoshihito Yoshida and former Wallaby wing Ian Williams, who is now working as a lawyer in Tokyo, are very dangerous, as is courageous fullback Takahiro Hosokawa.

WORLD CUP RESULTS

1987

USA	18 – 21
England	7 – 60
Australia	23 – 42

1991

Scotland	9 – 47
Ireland	16 – 32
Zimbabwe	52 – 8

Stern Competitors from Eastern Europe

ROMANIA

For many years, rugby's strength in Romania was that it was state sponsored. Under the repressive regime of Caeucescu, the game reflected the national mood and preoccupations. It was safety-first, forward-dominated and occasionally very effective, with several wins over France in the 1980s to show for their efforts.

By the time of the 1991 World Cup, though, the Romanians were no longer playing under orders, so to speak, and were desperately trying to expand and play a more exciting brand of 15-man running rugby. But it was an alien game to most of the players in Romania and it led to a number of heavy defeats in the run-up to the 1991 tournament, especially on their tour to New Zealand.

Although they beat only Fiji in 1991, they made much progress as a side and moved towards a game that was halfway between the expansive game they wished to play and the tight game they were good at. Ever gruelling up front, the Romanians took a heavy toll on opponents – Canadian Norm Hadley thought that the ultra-physical encounter with Romania's pack took more out of the Canucks than both of the other pool games put together.

A FEW BRIGHT SPOTS
The Romanians seemed to have arrived at a useful halfway house in

> *"The standard of the national side is far above their club rugby, but they do have the necessary skills to do well – and, the desire to use them."*
>
> **ROSS COOPER,**
> FORMER ROMANIAN COACH

Romania's scrum-half Daniel Neaga gets the ball away from a scrum.

terms of style. In 1994, Romania's pack dominated Wales in the World Cup qualifier in Bucharest, and but they lost to a last-minute try, and followed it with a disappointing short tour of England, primarily because of a disagreement between some of the more established players and the management which saw many of the best players omitted.

The Romanians have a tremendous pack, especially at the line-out where Constantin Cojacariu is one of the best middle of the line jumpers in the world. Yet for all that, Romania's qualification as the third European nation – Italy defeated them to qualify as Europe's second representative – means that they have been pitched into the so-called "Pool of Death" alongside Australia, Canada and hosts South Africa.

WORLD CUP RESULTS

1987

Zimbabwe	21 – 20
France	12 – 55
Scotland	28 – 55

1991

France	3 – 30
Canada	11 – 19
Fiji	17 – 15

Hard men from the Friendly Islands

TONGA

When the the game's governing body, invited 16 nations to the first World Cup, Tonga was one of the first "junior" nations to be pencilled in. But after a disappointing tournament in which they lost all three games – and were shocked to be comprehensively beaten by Canada – they failed to qualify for the 1991 tournament.

Western Samoa and Fiji were the two Pacific Island nations to play four years ago, Fiji by dint of their quarter-finalist status in 1987, and Western Samoa after they won the qualifying tournament. Now Fiji's decline as it increasingly focuses on sevens means it is Tonga's turn to have another chance to reaffirm their Test status.

The rivalry between the three countries always makes the triangular South Pacific Championship a fraught affair, especially now it is now also used as the quadrennial qualifying tournament for the World Cup. Indeed, so intense has the rivalry now become that the army have had to be called out three times in the last two years to keep the peace off the pitch.

PLAYER EXPORTERS

Tongans share the big-hitting mentality of their Samoan neighbours, although the most well-known exponent of their brand of rugby, Willie Ofahengaue, is now wearing a Wallaby shirt, while they have also lost several other top players – such as young back Semi Taupeafee – to Australia, New Zealand and Japan.

Even so, they still boast a formidable array of hard-running backs and forwards who will make a huge impact on the tournament. Some names to watch in particular are Samison Lola, a bustling 6ft 2in (1.89m) flanker from the Kolomatua club, as well as 22-year-olds Elisi Vunipola and lock Mateaki Mafi, the latter who is already attracting a good deal of attention from top Australian Rugby League clubs. Tonga will do well to keep hold of him – but even if they don't, there are few who will bet against them beating Ivory Coast and giving Scotland a very good run for their money in South Africa.

WORLD CUP RESULTS	
1987	
Canada	4 – 37
Wales	16 – 29
Ireland	9 – 32

> **"** Unlike Fiji, we are not immersed in the sevens culture. Fifteen-a-side is still dominant here, and that is why we have a better chance of success. **"**
>
> **DREW HAVEA,**
> TONGAN RFU SECRETARY

Tonga to the front – Tasi Vikilani on the charge against the Welsh tourists.

Rugby's Men from the Valleys Back on Song

WALES

The last four years have been the most depressing in Welsh rugby's proud history. The shock defeat on home soil by Western Samoa, coming as it did after 70-point defeats on their Australian tour, marked the lowest point in Welsh rugby history – worse even than the humiliating 1987 World Cup semi-final defeat at the hands of New Zealand.

With that as a background, it says much for coach Alan Davies and manager Bob Norster that Wales have managed to pull themselves back towards a position where they really can hope to compete effectively with the best in the world.

Although Five Nations Championship rugby is no real guide to world form, Wales can still point to winning the 1994–95 title – defeating France on the way – as evidence of a real revival. And as if that were not enough, they competed on equal terms with a hitherto rampant Springbok side just before Christmas 1994 and were unlucky to lose by 20–12. They can take heart from the facts that the pack was extremely competitive, especially at line-outs and scrums, and that they were without several key backs, all injured earlier in the year.

That performance was one of huge pride and showed that the appetite of the Welsh for their national game has not been dulled by a string of bad results. It hasn't helped that Wales has been dogged by misfortune since the beginning of 1994. First there were the raiding parties from Rugby League, who carried off two out of Wales's three 1993 British Lions as well as their brightest young forward prospect for many a year. Within the space of twelve months, centre Scott Gibbs, flanker Richard Webster and young number 8 Scott Quinnell entered the paid ranks and had ripped the heart out of a Welsh side that looked to be recovering well.

BAD BREAKS

As if that wasn't bad enough, Wales then suffered a spate of injuries in

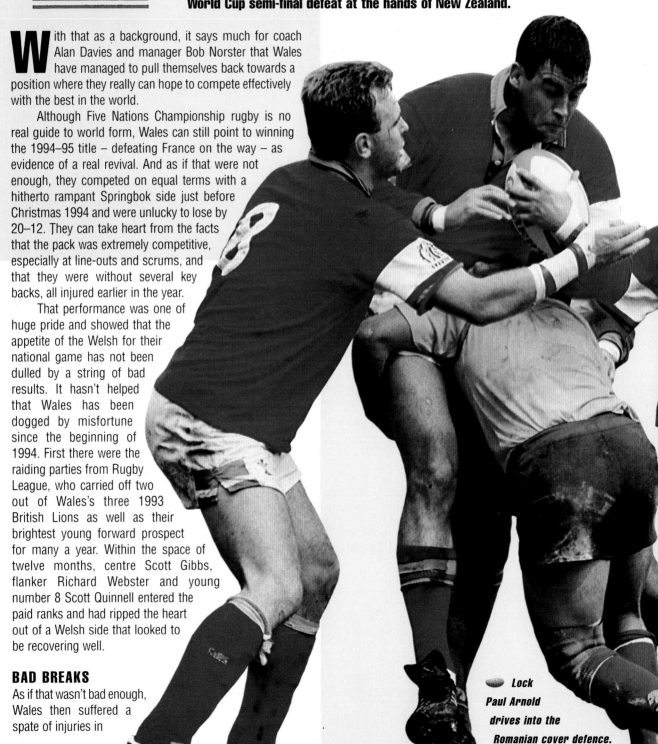

Lock Paul Arnold drives into the Romanian cover defence.

their back division. Captain and wing Ieuan Evans broke his ankle, fullback Mike Rayer broke his leg, while broken bones also sidelined wing Nigel Walker and centre Nigel Davies – four hugely influential players. Although only Rayer will miss the World Cup, the loss of that one player has seriously harmed Wales's cause.

Yet there is plenty of good news to set against the doom and gloom, particularly up front. As the Springboks found, the Welsh are very streetwise characters indeed, and nowhere is this more true than at the set-piece. They have developed a very strong front row of Mike Griffiths, Garin Jenkins and Ricky Evans, and consequently have a rock solid scrummage.

More importantly, Wales has a line-out team which at last competes for – and wins – its own ball. That is a novelty for them, and is largely due to the emergence of 6ft 10in (2.09m) lock Derwyn Jones, who had a superb debut against South Africa. As well as his own outstanding form, his arrival has also allowed Gareth Llewellyn to move back to the front of the line, where he is in imperious form. In addition, the impact of Hemi Taylor at the back of the line-out has made for a combative ball-winning unit.

Gareth Llewellyn takes the ball on in the World Cup qualifying campaign win over Romania.

BRITAIN'S BEST BACK DIVISION

Wales have the British Isles's most inventive back division. They may not be the best in defence, or be the quickest, yet the Welsh seem to be the one side in Britain which is consistently able to score tries. Although much of the reason for that may lie with the opposition they have been facing of late – Spain, Portugal, Romania, Italy, Canada, Fiji, Tonga and Western Samoa are not the best eight sides in the world – it is also true that the midfield partnership of Nigel Davies and Mike Hall are wonderfully experienced distributors of the ball and are capable of breaking down any defence.

In Ieuan Evans and Nigel Walker, Wales also have two of the speediest wings in the world. Walker, a former international sprinter, is particularly nippy, while Evans has proven himself a phenomenal try-scorer. That said, Wales's best chance of winning games – especially in the thin air of the Veldt, where the ball flies huge distances – is the boot of Neil Jenkins. The young fly-half is now arguably the best goal-kicker in the world, and he can – and will – punish indiscretions mercilessly.

> *"Welsh rugby has reached an important stage in its development. We know that we can rattle sides, but we must start winning. We must never forget that success breeds success."*
>
> **PHIL BENNETT,**
> LEGENDARY WELSH FLY-HALF

WORLD CUP RESULTS

1987

Ireland	13 – 6
Tonga	29 – 16
Canada	40 – 9
England *(Quarter-final)*	16 – 3
New Zealand *(Semi-final)*	6 – 49
Australia *(Play-off)*	22 – 21

1991

Western Samoa	13 – 16
Argentina	16 – 7
Australia	3 – 38

CHAPTER 4

The History of the
WORLD CUP

With hindsight, the decision to hold a World Cup for rugby was the perfect way to bring together the disparate strands of the game. Never before had all of the top nations got together in one place to finally determine which was the greatest side in the world. It had been the four British Unions which held out against the concept for years, rightly fearing that the tournament would inevitably accelerate the process of professionalising the game. But after long deliberation, John Kendall-Carpenter and the International Rugby Football Board finally took the gamble and, in 1987, the 16 invited nations arrived in Australia and New Zealand to contest the Webb Ellis Trophy, changing the face of the game for ever.

POOL ONE

Australia, England, Japan & USA

England faced the biggest pack Australia had ever fielded and emerged, if not unscathed, at least with honour. But with Lynagh, Papworth and Farr-Jones running riot, the Wallaby backs were an irresistible force, running out 19–6 winners thanks to tries by Campese and flanker Poidevin. The USA surprised everyone by beating Japan 21–18 to avoid a whitewash, but the two minnows were soundly beaten by England and Australia, conceding 183 points between them in four rather unbalanced pool matches.

POOL TWO

Canada, Ireland, Tonga & Wales

It was business as usual for the two Celtic cousins, Wales and Ireland, who engaged in a scrappy Five Nations-style encounter. Wales avenged their defeat of earlier that year, staging a second half performance that netted them all of their points in the 13–6 win, Mark Ring scoring the only try of the game. Tonga were the whipping boys of Pool Two, losing to an unconvincing Wales (29–16) and Ireland (32–9), while they were also comprehensively beaten by the powerful Canadians, losing 37–4.

POOL THREE

Argentina, Fiji, Italy & New Zealand

The tournament had a stunning start in Auckland, when the All Blacks mercilessly ripped Italy apart in the most awesome display of power rugby ever seen. John Kirwan's 80-metre dash through at least eight tackles was the highlight of a second half during which the All Blacks racked up 57 points in their record 70–6 win. They also demolished Fiji 74–13 and Argentina 46–15. Despite their mauling from New Zealand, Fiji also went through to the quarter-finals on points difference.

POOL FOUR

France, Romania, Scotland & Zimbabwe

France, playing Scotland, staged one of the more spectacular comebacks of the tournament, dragging themselves back from 16–6 down entering the final quarter, to lead 20–16 with one minute remaining. But with referee Fred Howard about to blow the final whistle, Scotland's wing Matt Duncan squeezed over to produce the only draw – 20–20 – of the competition. Zimbabwe and Romania suffered severe beatings, the worst of which were the Africans' 70–12 and 60–21 defeats by France and Scotland respectively.

Quarter-finals

New Zealand 30, Scotland 3

Lancaster Park, Christchurch

Seriously outgunned at the set-pieces, Scotland's backs hardly saw the ball all afternoon – and without possession, it is impossible to play. What Scotland did have to offer, though, was their willingness to tackle all afternoon, and it was a capacity that was necessary as they faced wave after wave of All Black attacks. The pressure eventually told and, early in the second half, flanker Alan Whetton drove over for the try that ended Scotland's resistance.

France 31, Fiji 16

Eden Park, Auckland

Fijian flair faced the harsh reality of the international rugby world when they were comprehensively outplayed by the fiery French in Auckland. With scrum-half Berbizier outstanding, France engaged in a battle of attrition with Fiji's pack, as the three tries scored by forwards Rodriguez and Lorieux testify. A further try by the "Bayonne Express", wing Patrice Lagisquet, saw France to a comfortable win.

Australia 33, Ireland 15

Concord Oval, Sydney

Unfortunately for Mick Doyle's Ireland side, the game was effectively over as a contest by the end of the first half. Ireland conceded 27 points and scored none, and by the time the Irish got the measure of the juggernaut Wallaby pack, they had already been completely overrun. Although Australia were outscored in the second half, such was the measure of their first half domination, that the result was rarely in doubt.

Wales 16, England 3

Ballymore Oval, Brisbane

No amount of passion could disguise the woefully poor standard of this rivalry-ridden game played in the searing Brisbane heat. England went into the game with high hopes after creditable Pool performances, but did not show enough form against a side which was eminently beatable. It was a passion-powered performance from Wales, who were by far the better team on the day. Wales outscored England by three tries to nil, with John Devereux's late touchdown from an interception emphatically confirming their domination.

Semi-finals

France 30, Australia 24

Concord Oval, Sydney

It ranks as the most momentous and entertaining World Cup game ever played. France, recognising the need to come out and discomfort the huge Australian pack, tore into the Wallabies from the opening kick-off. The impact was devastating, and produced one of the game's great contests. The Australians, who had marched relatively unhindered through the competition, found themselves in a desperate battle to reach the final. The lead changed hands six times and, as the game entered the final few minutes, the result was still in doubt. In the end, there was no answer to Blanco's sublime injury-time try, a piece of individual brilliance and flair the like of which the Concord Oval had not seen before or since.

New Zealand 49, Wales 6

Ballymore Oval, Brisbane

Wales had failed to impress overly during the tournament and had featured in two of the dullest games of the competition – against Ireland and England, although they did win both. Against New Zealand they were comprehensively outplayed in an embarrassing indictment of British rugby. Richards's dismissal with quarter of an hour to play was the final disgrace as New Zealand rolled relentlessly on, accumulating points at a steady rate throughout the one-sided affair. The gap between Northern and Southern Hemisphere rugby styles was made clearer when David Kirk said after the game: "We have got a lot of work to do. We were a bit sloppy." And he wasn't joking!

Third place play-off

Wales 22, Australia 21

International Stadium, Rotorua

The controversial dismissal of Australian flanker David Codey by referee Fred Howard after just four minutes gave Wales a head start which they accepted with gratitude. Both sides had been looking for a good performance in the play-off to try to dispel the memories of their respective semi-final defeats. But with Codey gone, a Jonathan Davies-inspired Wales rallied and – to their credit after a morale-sapping pummelling in the semi-final defeat by New Zealand – took the game to the Wallabies. Tries by flankers Roberts and Moriarty, plus another by Hadley, gave Wales the narrowest of wins.

Right: All Blacks number 8 Wayne Shelford dives in to halt the progress of French fullback Serge Blanco.

THE FINAL

After the exhilarating France vs. Australia semi-final, the main event was a profound disappointment. Efficiency may win trophies, but it is rarely beautiful, and the All Blacks were certainly efficient. There was a grimly meticulous approach to New Zealand's play, while the French looked spent and, if not disinterested, at least like men who had been drained by their emotional semi-final victory over Australia a few days earlier. As coach Jacques Fouroux said: "We played our final in Sydney."

But if the French were slightly ambivalent by the time the tournament's climax arrived, the same could not be said of the All Blacks. They were a side on a mission – not only to win the inaugural World Cup at home, but also to avenge their comprehensive defeat in Nantes a few months before the competition kicked off. As John Kirwan said: "The defeat in Nantes stuck in my mind all over the summer. We just didn't go forward that day – from the kick-off. All Blacks never forget. It's been a long, long summer remembering that and I'm glad we have the chance to even it up."

And even it up they did. Dominating the first half, New Zealand did what they do best, and drove countless times around the fringes. It was classic All Black rugby: disciplined, heads-down, all guts and determination. France defended resolutely, but were undone when Grant Fox's miscued drop-goal attempt fell for flanker Michael Jones to go over. Second-half tries from captain David Kirk and John Kirwan finally broke the French resistance, and settled the identity of the Webb Ellis Trophy's first winners. An injury-time try by Berbizier was little consolation for an exhausted French team.

Left: New Zealand captain David Kirk displays the spoils of the 1987 final victory over the French at Eden Park, Auckland, as he claims the first Webb Ellis Trophy.

20 JUNE 1987, AT EDEN PARK, AUCKLAND
ATTENDANCE: 48,035

New Zealand 29, France 9

- -

NEW ZEALAND
Gallagher; Kirwan, Stanley, Taylor, Green; Fox, Kirk (Capt.); McDowell, Fitzpatrick, Drake, Pierce, G. Whetton, A. Whetton, Jones, Shelford.

FRANCE
Blanco; Camberabero, Sella, Charvet, Lagisquet; Mesnel, Berbizier; Ondarts, Dubroca (Capt.), Garuet, Lorieux, Condom, Champ, Erbani, Rodriguez.

- -

SCORERS
NEW ZEALAND: Tries: Jones, Kirk, Kirwan; Con: Fox; Pens: Fox (4); DG: Fox.
FRANCE: Try: Berbizier; Con: Camberabero; Pen: Camberabero.

THE 1991 WORLD CUP *The Quest Continues*

If the 1987 tournament had set the ball rolling for the game, the 1991 version sent its popularity and profile into the stratosphere. Held in the world's most populous rugby region – the Five Nations Championship countries of England, Scotland, Wales, Ireland and France – the tournament took over life in Britain, giving the game a higher profile than it had ever enjoyed before. For better or worse, the quest for the World Cup had become international rugby's ultimate prize, and there could be no turning back. The World Cup had bcome the be-all and end-all.

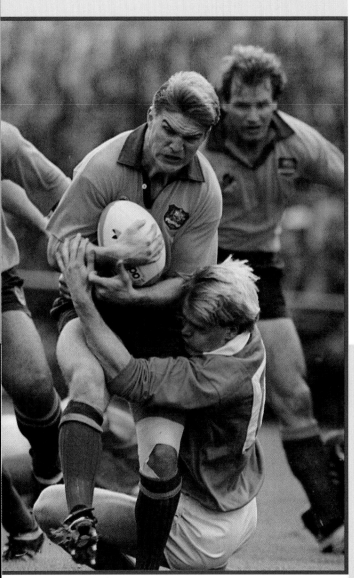

Outstanding Wallaby centre Tim Horan crashes into Ireland wing Simon Geoghegan in the Dublin quarter-final.

POOL ONE

New Zealand, England, Italy & USA

England versus New Zealand was the biggest draw outside the final stages and playing it on the first day guaranteed massive coverage. England lost a doggedly contested match, 18–12, when John Kirwan slipped Chris Oti's tackle to put in Michael Jones. Italy and the USA performed better than expected, with Italy giving New Zealand a harder time than they expected, before going down 31–21. They disappointed in the 36–7 loss to England, but atoned by beating the USA 30–9, with scrum-half Francescato outstanding.

POOL TWO

Scotland, Ireland, Japan & Zimbabwe

Scotland effectively won the easiest group in the tournament when they beat Ireland 24–15 at Murrayfield, the match marred by a disgraceful forearm smash from flanker Finlay Calder on Ireland's Jim Staples. Zimbabwe were the Pool's weakest team. Embarrassed 51–12 by Scotland and 55–11 by Ireland, they lost heavily to Japan in Belfast. The Africans recoiled in the face of wave after wave of frenetic attacks and were beaten 52–8.

POOL THREE

Australia, Wales, Argentina & Western Samoa

Talented but underestimated Western Samoa shocked Wales to win 16–13 at Cardiff, their dynamism and ferocious offensive tackling unsettling the Welsh. The Samoans' next game – against Australia in the mud and rain of Pontypool – was, despite Australia's 9–3 win, a classic and a moral victory for Samoa. Samoa's 35–12 victory over Argentina saw them into the quarter-finals, while Wales defeated the Pumas to avoid an embarrassing whitewash.

POOL FOUR

France, Fiji, Canada & Romania

Canada's awesome firepower was no secret, yet they almost shocked France. The French wilted under the onslaught, and only a moment of virtuosity from wing Philippe St Andre turned the tide. France progressed smoothly after beating Canada, easily defeating Romania, 30–3, and Fiji, 33–9. Romania shaded their meeting with Fiji, 17–15 – both lost to Canada – but they were limited sides; Fiji with a porous defence; while Romania offered little outside fly-half.

Samoan scrum-half Matthew Vaea takes on the Welsh.

Quarter-finals

England 19, France 10

Parc des Princes, Paris

Both sides had worked themselves up into a frenzy and in the brutal opening exchanges, the packs squared off after Nigel Heslop was floored by a flurry of blows. The rest of the match was a frenetic, torrid, bruising affair, with England just shading an uncompromising confrontation. England sealed the game well into the last quarter, Carling fielding a high ball and crashing over. It was all too much for French coach Daniel Dubroca, who manhandled referee David Bishop in the tunnel afterwards, losing his job in the acrimonious aftermath.

Scotland 28, Western Samoa 6

Murrayfield, Edinburgh

Coming into the match, all the talk had been of the Samoans' savage offensive tackling, yet on the day, it was Scotland's fullback Gavin Hastings whose charges around the fringes committed the Samoans and caused real damage. The Samoans just could not get into a game Scotland dominated. With the ball constantly moved away from the point of contact, the Samoans found Scottish targets hard to hit. Wings Iwan Tukalo and try-scorer Tony Stanger were outstandingly physical, as was flanker John Jeffrey, who claimed two tries.

Australia 19, Ireland 18

Lansdowne Road, Dublin

The game had gone pretty much as Ireland had planned. Their pack competed voraciously for every scrap of possession, but with five minutes to go, Australia were just ahead. Ireland, uncharacteristically and desperately, threw the ball around and scored a try that has gone down in Irish rugby folklore. The ball broke to flanker Gordon Hamilton who, with David Campese in pursuit and 50,000 screaming Irishmen willing him on, crashed over. Yet, in a staggering turnaround, with only seconds to go, Michael Lynagh started and finished off a move that ended with the winning try.

New Zealand 29, Canada 13

Stade du Nord, Lille

This was the match in which Canadian rugby came of age. Down by two tries early and 21–3 at half time, they fought back in a style which firmly established them in the top flight. The Canadian pack outscrummaged, outjumped, outrucked and outmauled the All Blacks, knocking them back in the tackle and consistently making ground with the ball in hand. The Canadians had seen this game as a rite of passage – and it was a test they passed in a memorable second half.

England's Paul Ackford takes clean line-out ball in the quarter-final against France at the Parc des Princes.

Semi-finals

England 9, Scotland 6

Murrayfield, Edinburgh

Despite their surfeit of possession, this was not an easy victory for an England side which dominated Scotland's forwards. The Scots creaked, wheeled, collapsed or buckled at every scrummage, allowing England to apply pressure throughout. Even the little possession that Scotland won from the lineout was bad ball, and this gave the English back row further opportunities to apply pressure to sorely harassed Scotland scrum-half, Gary Armstrong.

For all their possession, though, England were woefully poor at making best use of it. Scottish fullback Gavin Hastings had a mighty game in defence, fielding high kick after high kick. Indeed, Scotland's miserly defence never looked like being breached, and it was to the England back division's detriment that they had to rely on Andrew's late drop-goal – incredibly just six minutes from time – to secure a victory which their forwards had worked so hard for. And it should have been a lot worse; Gavin Hastings had missed a simple penalty a few minutes earlier.

Australia 16, New Zealand 6

Lansdowne Road, Dublin

This was David Campese's finest hour. Barely five minutes into the game, he came storming off his wing to score in the opposite corner as the All Blacks looked on in disbelief. Yet if that try surprised the New Zealanders, it was as nothing compared to his second decisive contribution to the game. With half-time looming, Campese broke clear and delivered a perfectly timed, outrageous, over-the-shoulder pass to team-mate Tim Horan who scored unchallenged.

Campese's intervention was a wonderful moment of individual skill which, along with Michael Lynagh's try against Ireland, were defining points in the Wallabies' campaign. That score put Australia 12 points clear, and New Zealand never recovered. Australia's first-half domination was so complete that New Zealand barely set foot in Wallaby territory and their kicker, Grant Fox, had not been given a chance to reply. Despite a stirring second-half display in which the All Black pack returned to their fierce driving pattern, Campese had effectively decided the game.

Third place play-off

New Zealand 13, Scotland 6

National Stadium, Cardiff

New Zealand gained a little consolation for the loss of their crown. Although they went behind early in the game, three penalties put them six points clear entering the final six minutes. In champions' style, they rebounded from Gavin Hastings's second penalty to score the game's only try three minutes later.

England's Paul Ackford dominates the Scottish line-out.

THE FINAL

Australian captain Nick Farr-Jones holds aloft the Webb Ellis Trophy after the 1991 World Cup final.

Rarely have statistics told the story of a game so precisely. England fly-half Rob Andrew received the ball 41 times and passed it 26; his Australian counterpart Michael Lynagh received it 17 times and passed it just four. England literally threw the game away.

For a side that had reached the World Cup final through a dogged ability to play to a limited game plan based on its strengths up front, this was a radical, ill-timed and ill-advised departure from the plan. It was as if the shortcomings that they displayed in the semi-final against Scotland just hadn't sunk in; England had not played an expansive game since their psychological battering at the hands of Scotland's Grand Slam-winning side of 1990, and were simply not accustomed to running the ball.

Hooker Brian Moore was just one of the forwards who confessed afterwards to being baffled by the tactics his side had used on the field. Coach Roger Uttley agreed: "We certainly did not intend to go out to run the ball all afternoon, and I think the guys on the pitch subconsciously yielded to the pressure from the press for a more expansive game."

Yet it was to the England forwards that the final belonged. They battered at the Wallaby defences for the whole 80 minutes, drawing a penalty tally of 15–8 in England's favour and completely dominating the much-vaunted Wallaby pack in the process.

Yet no matter how hard they banged on the Wallaby door, no matter how often they recycled possession, the ball they won was eventually spread wide where England's backs crashed against the impenetrable Australian back line. Centres Tim Horan and Jason Little were outstanding as Australia held on to the lead that prop Tony Daly's first half score had given them.

Right: Tony Daly's World Cup-winning try.

CHAPTER 5

Guide to
RUGBY LAWS & TACTICS

KEY TERMS & RUGBY JARGON

Commentators and TV pundits favour certain phrases, not all of which are self-explanatory. Here are a few of the more common expressions.

BLIND SIDE   Sometimes described as the short or narrow side. These are more precise definitions of the length of pitch from scrum, ruck or maul to the nearer touchline.

FAIR CATCH   See Mark

FIVE-METRE SCRUM   When a defending player takes the ball over his own try line and cannot bring the ball back into the field of play – either because of a tackle or running beyond the end-line, play restarts with a scrum five metres from that try line with the attacking team gaining the feed.

FEED/PUT-IN   When play restarts with either a line-out or scrum, the advantage goes to the team who puts the ball in play.

FREE KICK   An award for lesser offences than the full penalty. A team may neither put a free kick directly into touch from outside its 22, nor can it kick at goal from the hand or ground until after the ball has gone dead again or been touched by an opponent. It is also the kick that follows a successful Mark (see below).

GAIN LINE   An imaginary line from touchline to touchline that bisects the scrum, line-out, ruck and maul.

GRUBBER KICK   A bouncing ball kicked immediately into the ground. The grubber kick is difficult to judge and handle because the ball is likely to take a strange bounce.

THE LOOSE   This refers to rucks and mauls, which are also embraced by all phases of possession that follows first phase. i.e. second phase, third phase and so on. Not to use one phrase when three will do, rucks and mauls are also referred to as the breakdown. So if a commentator describes a player as "first to the breakdown" he is the first man to the ball when possession has to be recycled after a tackle.

MARK   Also known as a fair catch. A player who cleanly catches the ball direct from an opponent's kick within his own 22, with at least one foot on the ground may call for a mark, resulting in a free kick award.

NARROW SIDE   See Blind side

NO SIDE   The final whistle to end the half or game. It is always blown when play is dead, but never before a penalty kick is taken.

OPEN SIDE   The opposite to the blind side, it is the wider part of the field.

PEEL   A ball which is tapped from a line-out to another forward prior to him setting off round the back or front of the line-out.

PENALTY   Penalties are awarded for more serious offences than those that merit a free kick. The team awarded a penalty can kick at goal or kick for touch, in which case they get the feed at the resulting line-out.

SET PIECE   Also referred to as "first phase possession", the set piece encompasses scrummages and line-outs.

SHORT SIDE   See Blind side

TIGHT   The set-piece part of the game, i.e. the scrum and the line-out. The phrase "tight loose" is occasionally used. This refers to the stage when the rolling maul comes to resemble an impromptu scrum.

22 DROP-OUT   When a player grounds the ball behind his own line – usually following a missed kick – he touches the ball down and play restarts with a drop-out from his own 22-metre-line.

UP AND UNDER   Also called the bomb and the Garryowen – the latter after the Irish club of the same name – it is when the ball is kicked high in the air, allowing the attackers to engulf the catcher. If the catcher – normally a three-quarter or fullback – makes a fair catch inside his own 22-metre-line, he can call for a Mark.

LAWS

Rugby is essentially a simple game. Although many new laws have been introduced in recent times, these have been technical amendments more than anything else. These are not the laws as they are written but a guide to the game.

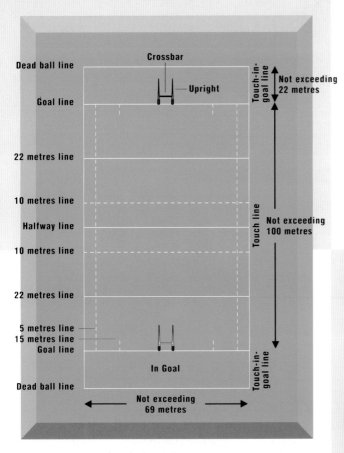

DIAGRAM 1 THE FIELD OF PLAY

THE TEAMS

The teams are made up of 15 players, and their formation is as follows: Fullback (number 15); the three-quarter line comprising two wings (14 and 11) and two centres, an inside and an outside (13 and 12); two half-backs, stand-off or fly-half (10) and scrum-half (9); and the pack. The pack – also known as forwards – contains the front row of two props, with the tighthead on the right and the loosehead on the left at the scrum (1 and 3) and the hooker (2), two second rows, also known as locks (4 and 5), two flankers, an open side flanker (who tends to be a smaller, faster player) and the blind side, who tends to be a bigger player, more suited to tackling and grappling (6 and 7) the man at the back (the number 8). These eight players form the scrum.

SCORING

There are four methods of scoring points: try (worth five points), conversion (two), penalty (three) and drop goal (three). A try is scored when an attacking player, while in control of the ball, grounds it between the goal line and the dead-ball (end) line. If the referee considers that the defending team deliberately commits an offence to prevent the attacking team from scoring a try, he may award a penalty try. Following a try, the scoring team then has the chance to kick at goal for a conversion, from the ground. The kick is taken from a point decided by the attacking team so long as it is from a spot parallel to the touchline in line with where the try was scored (allowing the kicker the most advantageous angle for his attempt - see Diagram 2). A conversion from a penalty try is from in front of the posts. As with all other scoring kicks, the ball must travel between the posts and over the crossbar, but it can hit the crossbar and/or the uprights before going through to count.

　　Penalties are kicked following various offences, such as serious foul play, offside and deliberate obstruction. Play is dead and the ball is kicked from the ground, and as with a conversion the player may improve his angle by moving the ball backwards (but parallel to the touchline) from the position of the offence. A drop goal may be kicked from anywhere in open play, the ball being dropped to the ground and kicked as it bounces.

KICK-OFF

Each half and play following a score starts with a kick-off from the centre point along the halfway line. If the ball fails to travel 10 metres before being touched by the kicking team or travels directly out of play, the non-kicking team has a choice of a scrum on halfway, allowing the kick to stand or receiving another kick-off. If a penalty occurs as a try is scored (such as a knee in the back) then the scoring side restarts with a penalty.

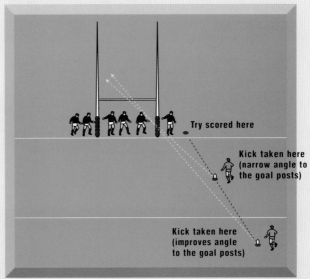

DIAGRAM 2 THE CONVERSION

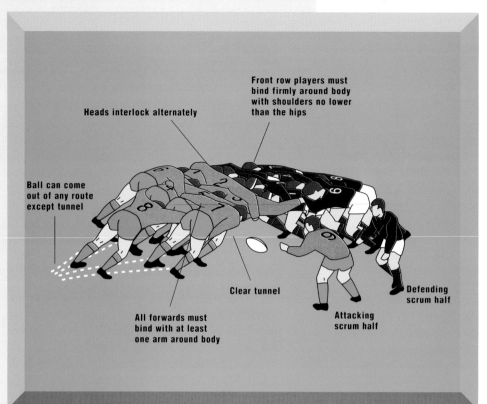

DIAGRAM 3 THE SCRUM

As soon as the two packs have bound in a scrum, the scrum-half must roll the ball into the channel between to two front rows. The hookers then use their feet to "hook" it back to their side. If the ball is not fed immediately or it goes towards his own forwards, the referee will award a free kick.

Heads interlock alternately

Front row players must bind firmly around body with shoulders no lower than the hips

Ball can come out of any route except tunnel

Clear tunnel

All forwards must bind with at least one arm around body

Attacking scrum half

Defending scrum half

DIAGRAM 4 THE LINE-OUT

There must be an equal number of men in the line-out (usually seven). The hooker throws the ball down the middle of the one-metre gap and the "jumpers" try to catch it. They can be "supported" (but not "lifted") by players, and must use their "inside arm" to catch the ball.

Players line up in single parallel lines

10 metres

Offside line for backs runs parallel to line-of-touch

Nearest player is 5 metres in

Team not throwing in the ball must not have more players in line-out than team throwing the ball

Clear space 1 metre between two lines of players

Ball must be thrown in at least 5 metres along line-of touch

Each team must have at least two players in the line-out

Player stands in touch at place marked by the touch judge

SCRUM DOWN

The scrum (see Diagram 3) is formed when the referee sees a technical or accidental offence. The penalised team is likely to lose possession as the opponents have the benefit of the put-in or feed. The scrum-half rolls the ball into the channel formed between the opposing front rows, often working on an agreed signal. When the ball enters the scrum, the hooker (in the middle of the front row) attempts to kick it back with his heel and the ball is then worked back for the scrum-half (or the number 8) to pick it up and start an attack.

LINE-OUT

When the ball or ball-carrier touches the side line between the try lines, a line-out is awarded where the ball goes out of play (see Diagram 4). The exception here is if the ball is kicked from outside the kicker's 22-metre area in open play over the touchline without bouncing. Then the line-out takes place level with where the ball was kicked. The line-out throw gives the advantage to the team not in possession and the throwing team has the option of choosing the number of players in the line, up to a maximum of seven. The ball must be thrown in a straight line between the two sets of players, the first man who must be five metres from the line and the teams two metres apart. If the throw is not straight the non-feeding team can choose between either a line-out or scrum with their feed. If the ball is kicked directly into touch from a penalty, the kicking side also throws-in at the line-out. The ball can go straight into touch from a penalty (without bouncing first).

RUCK/MAUL

Rucks and mauls form when the ball-carrier is tackled and the two teams battle for possession. When the ball-carrier remains standing in the tackle, a maul forms, but if the ball is on the ground a ruck is formed. The difference between a ruck and maul is vital, because it determines who gets the put-in at the scrum if the ball does not emerge. If a ruck has formed, the team which took the ball into contact (i.e. the team whose player was tackled) gets the feed at the scrum. If the player who took the ball into contact, however, stays on his feet (i.e. a maul develops), then the ball must come out, or the put-in at the scrum will go to the defending team (i.e. the tackling team). This is why a tackled player will try to "go to ground" if he is not able to pass the ball immediately he is tackled.

RELEASING THE BALL

When the ball-carrier is tackled he does not have to release the ball as long as he is still standing. Once he is taken to the ground, he must release the ball and get to his feet before he can play it again. Failure to do so results in a penalty to the defending team.

KNOCK-ON/FORWARD PASS

If a player in possession mishandles the ball and it falls forward to the ground, he shall be penalised by the award of a scrum with the opposing team gaining the advantage of feeding the ball. Similarly, if the ball is passed in a forward direction then a scrum is awarded again with defending team (the one not in possession) getting the put-in.

DIAGRAM 5 OFFSIDE

Player A1 kicks the ball then runs downfield (A2) and because he is in front of the ball the tackler (B) is onside, so can catch the ball or legally tackle the opponent. If the kicker had not run forward he would have been offside until the ball carrier had gone 10 metres.

ADVANTAGE

The referee can delay the award of a penalty or scrum if he feels the infringed against team can gain a clear advantage. He will signal with his arm that if no advantage accrues, then the offence will be penalised upon blowing his whistle.

OFFSIDE

The offside law is extremely complicated and subject to much argument. However, the rudiments are that if a player from either side is front of the ball from his perspective he cannot make a play for it either on the ground or by tackling an opponent. At a line-out, both teams not directly involved must remain 10 metres from the ball until it emerges into play, unless play is less than 10 metres from either try-line; then the defending team can move up to the try-line. If a player goes moves in front of the ball (described by commentators as "going over the top"), then he is offside. When a ball is kicked downfield everybody who is in front of the kicker at the moment of impact is offside unless the kicker runs in front of, or gathers, the ball (see Diagram 5). Otherwise the receiver must be allowed to run 10 metres. There is no offside in "broken play" when there is no scrum, maul, line-out, ruck or tackle situation.

In most cases of offside a penalty is awarded, but if a player in an offside position is accidentally struck by the ball or man in possession, then the referee may award a scrum.

DISSENT AND RETALIATION

If the referee feels a side have obstructed the quick taking of a penalty, or talked back to him, he may move the penalty forward 10 metres. It is unusual for him to move one penalty more than 10 metres, but not impossible. Retaliation by the side awarded a penalty after the award can also result in it being reversed, so that the other side gains the ball. A knee in the back as player goes over for a try can also bring a penalty restart.

TACTICS

Rugby tactics have undergone a huge evolution over the last 25 years. They have gone from the days when a team got to know each other a couple of hours before the kick-off to a series of endless pre-match meetings to shape every play according to the area of the pitch and the type of ball received. Legend has it that Ray Prosser, the former coach of the forward dominated Pontypool side of the 1970s, used to tell his players; "Occasionally the scrum-half will have to pass to his fly-half and that can't be helped. But when the ball goes to the inside centre, that's a move and I hate moves."

Here are two stories which successively support and contradict the philosophy that tactics are vital to successful rugby. Rugby being such a multi-faceted game, both following the game plan and 'freelancing' can work equally well in the heat of a game.

In the quarter-final of the 1991 World Cup, Australia were seconds away from going out to Ireland. Michael Lynagh gathered his team together, but there was no macho talk of "Right back at them boys". He told them he would kick off deep and the team had to keep Ireland down there. When they regained possession they would run a particular back move that they had practised hundreds of times in training. A minute later they had scored the game-winning try.

In an encounter in November 1994, South Africa had a scrum on the Scotland 22-metre-line, and called a back move to the open side. When the ball emerged their back row moved off in anticipation of where the ball was supposed to go and the Scottish defence made a similar assumption. Scrum-half Joost van der Westhuizen saw that a huge gap had been left, opted to cancel the move and scooted up the blind side to score without a hand being laid on him.

AUSTRALIA'S FLAT LINE ATTACK

Winners of the 1991 World Cup, Australia have developed into the major world force over the past 15 years. The key to their success is that they play a flat back line in which the players are interchangeable. Simply, the playmaker (usually the fly-half) stands right up in the faces of the defence with two other gifted distributors outside him. The other attackers run into the holes where the defence is weakest. By standing so flat, the Australians commit the defence, which has little time to adjust to make the tackle on the runner coming in.

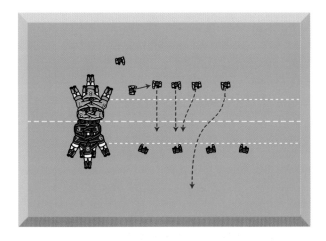

Australia's flat-line attack is intended to draw defenders too close to the point of attack and this then allows either the stand-off to kick past defenders for the three-quarters to chase downfield or for a rapid passing movement to find a hole in the defensive line. The Wallabies' three-quarter line is one of the best in the world and this system, prompted by their brilliant fly-half Michael Lynagh, allows them full rein to show off their speed, flair and strength. From the above position, if Lynagh was to run around the centres, or if the fullback joined the line of attack then the defending line would be outnumbered and the best outcome for the blue-shirted players from here would be a loss of position, though conceding five or seven points from a try is far more likely.

STRAIGHTENING THE LINE

In order to 'stand up' the drift defence, it is vital that someone straightens the attacking line, and the most obvious way is for attackers to run straight. Too often a fly-half, who needs time to play and consequently stands too deep, moves across to escape the opposition back row which pushes his back line across the field. Yet this initial move can be straightened by a flat short pass which allows the outside man to straighten his running angle. This pass can also be delivered to the blind-side wing coming inside to create an extra man and straighten the line. Similarly, a scissors pass (a pass delivered as the outside man crosses back behind the ball carrier) creates a new angle for the recipient to straighten the line.

THE ROLLING MAUL

In forward exchanges, the defence can force the forwards to release the ball if they can isolate the man in possession. To counter this packs will use the rolling maul. The scrum-half is the eyes and voice of this, instructing his forwards where the defence is at its weakest. His pack will consequently smuggle the ball to the forward at the point of weakness, gather round him, and roll off in a wedge driven through the opposition defence.

FORWARDS BREACHING THE GAIN LINE

The scrum-half passes to a forward standing out from a ruck or maul. He runs at the fringe defence, committing tacklers, and if he is stopped he should be able to pop up a pass for another driving forward to sustain the momentum. Good support play and quick ball are vital, but if well executed, sufficient tacklers have been taken out of the game to create room for the backs outside.

MAN-TO-MAN DEFENCE

The original defence was a strict man-to-man line, where wingers, centres, half-backs and forwards cancelled each other out, with the full-back assisting where necessary, but as players have become fitter, this method has fallen into disuse and has been replaced by the "drift defence".

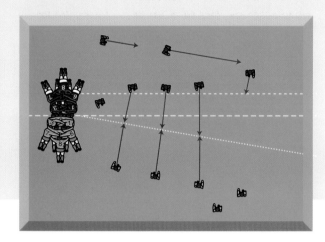

The man-to-man marking system is the easiest defence to operate. In this defence each of the backs has a particular player to mark, as follows: scrum-half on scrum-half, fly-half on fly-half, left wing on right wing, left centre on right centre, right centre on left centre and right wing on left wing. The fullback does not actually mark his opposite number, but he covers the space behind the line and will take on a man coming through the line. If the fullback comes into the line too quickly he may well find himself right out of position should the ball be kicked ahead. The problem with the man-to-man defence is that if it is too rigid, then moves such as the missed man, or a loop or scissors will create a big hole in the line as the defence over-commits.

DRIFT DEFENCE

The "drift defence" is still the most popular defensive formation. It was originally designed to prevent the attack from creating a numerical advantage by bringing the full-back into the line. The basis is for the defending flanker to get a line on the opposition fly-half, allowing the three-quarters to drift one man across – the fly-half on to the inside centre, inside

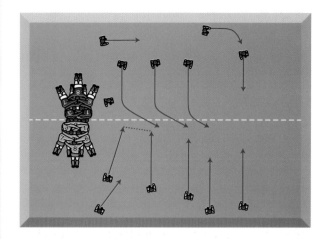

The drift or sliding defence has become by far the most popular in recent years. It is the most convenient way of forcing the attackers to go across the field rather than forward. It is a modified form of the man-to-man system, but the defending three-quarters move across one position, so that the last pass will put the attacking winger in a situation where he is faced by both the opposite winger and the centre with very limited space to work. Unless this winger has fantastic pace he won't be able to go around the outside of the markers and is going to be hemmed in by the touchline and the defenders, leaving him with little option but to either reverse his field or to kick ahead, which will result in either a loss of position or possession.

on to outside centre and so on. The defender then attacks the inside shoulder of the ball-carrier, forcing the attacking line to go across the field towards the touchline. Eventually, the attacking wing will end up pinned to the touchline hopelessly outnumbered by defending backs.

TACTICAL KICKING

In defence there are two basic kicks. The traditional favourite is the long boot to find touch, which clears the immediate danger and allows the defence to regroup, but this has been supplemented by the high, infield kick which doesn't concede the line-out – and probable possession – but forces the attackers to build again.

In attack the long-range favourites are the high ball or 'bomb' hoisted towards the fullback or wing. If the ball is being moved down the line and the defence is up very flat (in a straight line across the pitch) a short chip over the top or a grubber into a gap is an effective way of getting behind them. Other options are the crossfield kick for the open side wing, or a variety of scrum-half kicks to put pressure on the defending blind side wing.

The long downfield kick can, however, lead to some pretty boring games of "aerial ping-pong". This tactic is often favoured by sides which have a weak scrummage, and has been used to good effect in recent times by Scotland.

FINAL
WHISTLE

The teams have been introduced to the assembled dignitaries; the national anthems have been sung; the *haka* has been performed and other ritual pleasantries exchanged... it's time for the toughest guys in world sport to get the job done (and they'll be singing in the bars of Abidjan/Alice Springs/Apia/Auckland/Bath/Bucharest/Dax/Hawick/Limerick/Milan/Pontypridd/Rosario/Stellenbosch/Tokyo/Tongatapu/Vancouver tonight*).

*Please delete where applicable!

PICTURE ACKNOWLEDGEMENTS
The publishers would like to thank the following sources for their kind permission to reproduce the pictures in this book:

Allsport: Clive Brunskill. Simon Bruty. David Cannon. Russell Cheyne. Mike Hewitt. David Rogers. Anton Want: **Audience Planners/South African Tourist Office**: **Colorsport**: Colin Elsey. Stephen Louwrens: **Robert Harding Picture Library**: Sporting Pictures. **Bob Thomas Sports Photography**.

Every effort has been made to acknowledge correctly and contact the source and/or copyright holder of each picture, and Carlton Books Limited apologises for any unintentional errors or omissions, which will be corrected in future editions of this book.